MELISA'S TRAVEL GUIDES

Spain Travel Guide 2023

The Best Places to Visit, Things to Do, and Tips for Planning Your Trip | Everything You Need to Know to Plan Your Dream Vacation to Spain

Copyright © 2023 by Melisa's Travel Guides

All rights reserved. No part of this publication may be reproduced, stored or transmitted in any form or by any means, electronic, mechanical, photocopying, recording, scanning, or otherwise without written permission from the publisher. It is illegal to copy this book, post it to a website, or distribute it by any other means without permission.

First edition

This book was professionally typeset on Reedsy.
Find out more at reedsy.com

Contents

1	Welcome to Spain	1
2	Planning Your Trip to Spain	4
3	Essential Travel Information for Your Trip to Spain	8
4	Exploring Spanish Culture and History	12
5	Top Cities and Regions to Visit in Spain	16
6	Madrid: The Epitome of Spanish Grandeur and Cultural...	20
7	Barcelona: The Cosmopolitan Gem	23
8	Seville: Flamenco and Moorish Heritage	27
9	Valencia: A Fusion of Tradition and Modernity	30
10	Granada: The Alhambra and Moorish Splendor	34
11	Bilbao: Art, Architecture, and Gastronomy	37
12	Malaga and the Costa del Sol: Sun, Sea, and Culture	40
13	The Canary Islands: An Exquisite Tropical Utopia of...	44
14	The Balearic Islands: Mediterranean Beauty	47
15	Northern Spain: Green Landscapes and Coastal Charm	51
16	Southern Spain: Andalusian Delights	54
17	Basque Country: An Exquisitely Distinct Cultural Odyssey	57
18	Day Trips and Excursions	60
19	Exploring the Plethora of Outdoor Pursuits in Spain: A...	64
20	Spanish Cuisine and Gastronomy	67
21	Festivals and Celebrations in Spain: A Vibrant Tapestry of...	70
22	Shopping in Spain: A Multifaceted Retail Extravaganza	73
23	Practical Tips for Travelers	78
24	Language and Communication	83
25	Transportation in Spain	89

26	Exploring the Varied Landscape of Accommodation Options in...	93
27	Ensuring Safety and Security: An In-Depth Guide for...	97
28	Sustainable Travel in Spain	101
29	Spain for Budget Travelers	105
30	Unforgettable and Transformative Experiences Await You in...	110
31	Conclusion	114

1

Welcome to Spain

Spain, situated in the south-western corner of Europe, is a country that is renowned for its rich history, diverse culture, stunning landscapes, and vibrant cities. From the sun-kissed beaches of the Costa del Sol to the architectural wonders of Barcelona and the lively streets of Madrid, Spain has something to offer for all kinds of travelers.

Geographically, Spain is located on the Iberian Peninsula, with Portugal to the west and France to the northeast. It also includes the Balearic Islands in the Mediterranean Sea and the Canary Islands off the northwest coast of Africa. The country is blessed with a varied terrain, from the rugged mountains of the Pyrenees and Sierra Nevada to the vast plains and picturesque coastal regions.

Spain has a long and fascinating history that has shaped its present-day cultural identity. The Iberian Peninsula has been inhabited since prehistoric times, and throughout its history, Spain has seen the rise and fall of various civilizations. From the Phoenicians, Romans, and Moors to the medieval kingdoms and the Spanish Empire, each era has left its mark on the country's architecture, traditions, and art.

The culture of Spain is a delightful tapestry of influences from different regions and historical periods. Flamenco, the passionate and soul-stirring dance form, originated in Andalusia and has become synonymous with Spanish culture. Bullfighting, although controversial, is still an integral part of the Spanish tradition. Festivals such as La Tomatina and the Running of the Bulls showcase the country's love for celebration and revelry.

Spanish cuisine is renowned worldwide for its delectable flavors and diverse ingredients. Each region has its own culinary specialties, but some iconic dishes are universally loved. From paella, a rice dish infused with saffron and various seafood or meats, to tapas, small plates of appetizers that allow you to sample a variety of flavors, Spain offers a gastronomic journey like no other. Don't forget to pair your meals with the country's famous wines, including Rioja, Ribera del Duero, and Cava.

When it comes to exploring Spain, the country has an abundance of attractions and destinations. Madrid, the capital city, is a bustling metropolis that houses world-class museums like the Prado Museum, Reina Sofia Museum, and Thyssen-Bornemisza Museum. Barcelona, on the other hand, entices visitors with its unique blend of Gothic and modernist architecture, including the iconic Sagrada Familia and Park Güell.

The southern region of Andalusia is renowned for its enchanting cities, such as Seville, Granada, and Cordoba. Seville boasts the largest Gothic cathedral in the world, the Seville Cathedral, as well as the Alcázar, a stunning royal palace with lush gardens. Granada is home to the majestic Alhambra, a UNESCO World Heritage site, and Cordoba is known for the awe-inspiring Mezquita, a mosque-turned-cathedral.

The coastal regions of Spain, including the Costa del Sol, Costa Brava, and Costa Blanca, offer picturesque beaches, vibrant nightlife, and a relaxed Mediterranean atmosphere. These areas are popular among tourists seeking sun, sea, and sand.

For nature lovers, Spain has a variety of landscapes that range from the snow-capped peaks of the Sierra Nevada to the verdant forests of the Picos de Europa and the volcanic landscapes of the Canary Islands. The Camino de Santiago, a famous pilgrimage route, attracts hikers and spiritual seekers from around the world, while the national parks like Doñana and Teide provide opportunities for wildlife enthusiasts and outdoor adventurers.

In recent years, Spain has also become a hub for avant-garde architecture, with iconic buildings designed by renowned architects such as Antoni Gaudí, Santiago Calatrava, and Frank Gehry. The Guggenheim Museum in Bilbao, designed by Gehry, has become an architectural marvel and a symbol of the city's transformation.

Spain is a country that captivates the hearts of travelers with its rich history, diverse culture, stunning landscapes, and vibrant cities. Whether you're exploring the historic streets of Madrid, indulging in the flavors of Andalusian cuisine, or basking in the sun on the beaches of the Mediterranean, Spain offers an unforgettable experience that will leave you wanting more. So grab your bags, immerse yourself in the Spanish way of life, and embark on a journey of discovery in the captivating land of Spain.

2

Planning Your Trip to Spain

Planning a journey to Spain can be an energizing and compensating encounter. With its rich history, vivid culture, amazing engineering, and differing scenes, Spain has something for each sort of explorer. In any case, to make the most of your visit, it's essential to design ahead and think about various parts of your outing. In this part, we will manage you through the cycle of arranging your outing to Spain, covering all that you need to know from picking the correct time to visit, getting fundamental travel archives, making a schedule, and that's just the beginning. So how about we plunge in and begin arranging your remarkable experience to Spain!

1. Choosing the Right Time to Visit:

Spain encounters a scope of atmospheres and climate conditions all through the year, so it's essential to consider the best time to visit dependent on your inclinations and interests. The nation can be isolated into a few areas, each with its own one of a kind atmosphere. The mid year months (June to August) will in general be hot, particularly in focal and southern Spain, while the winter months (December to February) can be cold, particularly in the northern areas and higher heights. Spring (March to May) and harvest time (September to November) by and large offer pleasant temperatures and fewer groups, making them ideal for investigating well known vacationer goals.

2. Setting a Budget:

Before jumping into the subtleties of your outing, it's basic to set up a financial plan that suits your money related capacities. Spain caters to a wide scope of financial plans, from extravagance facilities and top of the line eateries to spending plan cordial alternatives, for example, hostels and reasonable nearby eateries. Consider the expenses of flights, convenience, transportation, suppers, exercises, and keepsakes when making your financial plan. It's additionally worth looking into and looking at costs for various attractions and administrations to guarantee you make the most financially savvy decisions during your outing.

3. Obtaining Travel Documents:

In the event that you're arranging an outing to Spain, ensure that you have all the fundamental travel archives all together. Residents of numerous nations require a substantial identification to enter Spain, with a base legitimacy of six months past the date of takeoff. Contingent upon your nationality, you may likewise need to acquire a visa before your outing. It's prudent to check the prerequisites and guidelines well ahead of time and permit adequate opportunity for the application cycle if necessary.

4. Researching and Creating an Itinerary:

Spain offers a wealth of attractions and goals, making it essential to lead exhaustive exploration and make a schedule that suits your interests and time limitations. Consider the term of your outing and prioritize the spots you might want to visit. A portion of the must-see goals in Spain incorporate Madrid, Barcelona, Seville, Valencia, Granada, Bilbao, and the Balearic and Canary Islands. Research the primary attractions, social occasions, and nearby celebrations occurring during your visit to make the most of your time in each area.

5. Transportation in Spain:

Spain brags a productive and very much associated transportation framework, making it moderately simple to explore the nation. Contingent upon your schedule and inclinations, you can pick between various methods of transportation, including homegrown flights, trains, transports, and rental vehicles. Local flights are the quickest approach to cover long separations, while trains offer a picturesque and agreeable travel experience. Transports are a financially savvy alternative for shorter separations and arriving at littler towns and towns. Renting a vehicle gives the adaptability to investigate off-the-beaten-way goals at your own pace.

6. Accommodation Options:

Spain offers a wide scope of convenience alternatives to suit various financial plans and inclinations. From extravagance lodgings and boutique facilities to spending plan cordial hostels and get-away rentals, there's something for everybody. Consider the area, courtesies, and surveys when picking your convenience. It's prudent to book ahead of time, particularly during pinnacle traveler seasons, to secure the best arrangements and accessibility.

7. Discovering Spanish Cuisine:

If you're a foodie, you'll love the flavors and regional dishes of Spanish cuisine. From tapas and paella to pintxos and seafood, there's something for everyone. Before you go, research the local specialties in each region you plan to visit and make a list of restaurants or food markets you want to try. Don't forget to sample the regional wines and the world-famous Jamón ibérico.

8. What to Pack:

When packing for your trip to Spain, think about the season and activities you plan to do. Pack comfortable shoes for walking, lightweight and breathable clothing for the summer, and layers for cooler evenings or winter visits. Don't forget the essentials like sunscreen, a hat, a reusable water bottle, and a universal power adapter.

9. Learning Basic Spanish Phrases:

If you're travelling to a Spanish-speaking area, it's always a good idea to learn a few basic phrases. Not only will it make your trip more enjoyable, but it will also show the locals that you respect their culture. Knowing some common greetings, expressions, and polite phrases will help you to make connections with the people you meet. Even if English is widely spoken in tourist areas, speaking a few words of Spanish will greatly enhance your travel experience.

10. Health and Safety:

Organizing a trip to Spain is an exciting experience that will create lasting memories. To make sure your journey is as smooth as possible, it's important to consider the best time to visit, set a budget, get the necessary travel documents, plan an itinerary, research transportation options, select accommodations, sample the local cuisine, pack the essentials, and learn some basic Spanish phrases.

Most importantly, prioritize your health and safety by taking the necessary precautions before and during your trip. Make sure you have travel insurance that covers medical emergencies and familiarize yourself with local healthcare facilities. Additionally, stay informed of any travel advisories or safety recommendations from your government and practice general safety measures such as being aware of your belongings and avoiding isolated or dimly lit areas, especially at night. Now that you have all the information you need, it's time to start planning and get ready to explore the wonders of Spain!

3

Essential Travel Information for Your Trip to Spain

When you are getting ready for a trip to Spain, it is important to have all the necessary information to make sure your journey is pleasant and stress-free. This chapter will provide you with helpful advice on the key elements of traveling to Spain, such as visa requirements, currency and money matters, healthcare and safety, communication, and transportation options. By being aware of these essential details, you will be ready to make the most of your time in Spain.

1. Visa Requirements:

Before you plan a trip to Spain, it is important to be aware of the visa requirements based on your nationality. As a member of the Schengen Area, Spain allows visitors from many countries to enter without a visa for short stays. Citizens of the European Union, the United States, Canada, Australia, and many other countries typically enjoy visa-free travel for up to 90 days within a 180-day period. However, it is advisable to check with the Spanish embassy or consulate in your home country to make sure you have the latest information and to confirm any specific requirements.

2. Currency and Money Matters:

The official currency of Spain is the Euro (€). It is recommended to exchange your currency for Euros before your trip or upon arrival at airports, banks, or exchange offices. Credit and debit cards are widely accepted throughout the country, but it's a good idea to carry some cash for small purchases and in case you come across establishments that do not accept cards. ATMs are readily available in major cities and towns, allowing you to withdraw cash conveniently. Be mindful of transaction fees and inform your bank of your travel plans to avoid any issues with card usage.

3. Healthcare and Safety:

Spain has excellent healthcare facilities, making it relatively safe for travelers. However, it is recommended to have travel insurance that covers medical expenses and emergency evacuation. If you are an EU citizen, make sure to obtain a European Health Insurance Card (EHIC) before your trip to benefit from the same healthcare rights as Spanish nationals. Non-EU citizens should check if their travel insurance provides sufficient coverage in Spain.

In terms of safety, Spain is generally considered safe for tourists. Like in any destination, it is wise to take precautions such as safeguarding your belongings, being aware of your surroundings, and avoiding isolated areas, especially at night. It is always helpful to familiarize yourself with emergency contact numbers and the location of the nearest embassy or consulate.

4. Communication:

Spanish is the official language of Spain, and while English is spoken in many tourist areas, it is beneficial to learn some basic Spanish phrases to make communication with locals easier. Language translation apps can also be useful tools during your trip. Additionally, having a pocket dictionary or phrasebook can be helpful for understanding signs, menus, and other written information.

5. Transportation Options:

Spain offers various transportation options to explore the country. The most common means of intercity travel is by train, with Spain's extensive railway network connecting major cities and regions. Renfe is the national train operator, offering both high-speed AVE trains and regional services. It is advisable to book train tickets in advance, especially during peak travel seasons.

Another popular mode of transport is buses, with several companies providing domestic routes throughout Spain. Buses are often more affordable than trains and can be a convenient option for shorter distances or reaching remote areas not easily accessible by rail.

For local transportation within cities, public transportation systems are efficient and reliable. Major cities have well-developed metro (subway) networks, trams, and buses. Taxis are also widely available, but it's essential to ensure they are licensed and use a meter or negotiate the fare beforehand.

6. Climate and Weather:

Spain has diverse climates due to its geographical location, with Mediterranean, Continental, and Oceanic climates being the most common. The weather can vary significantly depending on the region and season. It is advisable to check the weather forecast for your specific destination and pack accordingly. Summers can be hot, especially in the central and southern regions, while winters can be mild in most areas but colder in the north and mountainous regions.

7. Customs and Etiquette:

Understanding the local customs and etiquette can enhance your travel experience in Spain. Spanish people are generally warm and friendly, appreciating basic courtesy and politeness. It is common to greet people with a handshake or a kiss on both cheeks, depending on the region and familiarity. Tipping is not obligatory but is appreciated for excellent service. It is customary to round up the bill or leave a small tip in restaurants, cafes, and taxis.

8. Time Zone:

Spain is located in the Central European Time (CET) zone. During daylight saving time, Spain switches to Central European Summer Time (CEST), which is one hour ahead of CET. Make sure to adjust your clocks accordingly to avoid any confusion or missed appointments.

By familiarizing yourself with essential travel information, you are equipped with the necessary knowledge to plan and enjoy your trip to Spain. Remember to check visa requirements, handle currency matters, ensure appropriate healthcare coverage, practice safety precautions, and have a basic understanding of the local language and customs. By being well-prepared, you can make the most of your time in Spain and create unforgettable memories during your travels.

4

Exploring Spanish Culture and History

Situated in the south-western corner of Europe, Spain is a vibrant and diverse country with a rich cultural heritage and a captivating history that has left its mark on the world. From its ancient roots to its modern-day contributions, Spain has a unique legacy that continues to shape its people and customs. In this chapter, we will explore the fascinating world of Spanish culture and history, including its art, music, dance, literature, architecture, and more.

1. Ancient Beginnings:

To comprehend Spanish culture and history, we must go back to its ancient beginnings. Traces of human presence in the Iberian Peninsula date back over 35,000 years, with the Iberians, Celts, Phoenicians, Greeks, and Carthaginians all leaving their mark before the Roman conquest in 218 BC. The Romans had a major impact on Spain's infrastructure, language (Latin), and legal systems.

2. The Moorish Impact:

One of the most important chapters in Spanish history is the Moorish period. The Moors, a Muslim population from North Africa, invaded the Iberian Peninsula in the 8th century and established Al-Andalus, a Muslim territory that flourished for centuries. This period saw a flourishing of arts, sciences, and architecture, with iconic landmarks like the Alhambra in Granada and the Great Mosque of Cordoba being prime examples. The Moorish influence is still evident in Spanish culture, particularly in Andalusia, where elements of Islamic art and architecture continue to inspire.

3. Spanish Golden Age:

The 16th and 17th centuries marked Spain's Golden Age, a period of immense cultural and artistic accomplishments. This era saw the reign of powerful monarchs such as Isabella and Ferdinand, Charles V, and Philip II, who supported the arts and renowned artists like El Greco, Diego Velázquez, and Francisco de Zurbarán. The Spanish Golden Age also gave rise to one of the most influential writers in the Spanish language, Miguel de Cervantes, and his masterpiece, Don Quixote.

4. Flamenco: The Soul of Spain:

Flamenco, the passionate and soulful art form that combines singing (cante), guitar playing (toque), and dancing (baile), is synonymous with Spanish culture. Originating in Andalusia, flamenco is deeply rooted in the experiences of the gitanos (Romani people) and the cultural fusion of the Moorish, Jewish, and Gypsy communities. Flamenco conveys a range of emotions, from joy to sorrow, and its rhythmic beats and intense performances continue to captivate audiences around the world.

5. Spanish Cuisine and Wine:

No exploration of Spanish culture is complete without savoring its culinary delights. Spanish cuisine is renowned for its diverse flavors and regional specialties. From tapas (small plates) to paella (rice dish), and from Jamón Ibérico (Iberian ham) to churros (fried dough pastries), Spain offers a gastronomic journey for food lovers. Each region has its own culinary traditions and local dishes to explore. Spanish wine, including the world-famous Rioja and Cava, also holds a prominent place in the country's culture, with vineyards dotting the landscapes.

6. Festivals and Celebrations:

Spain is famous for its lively festivals and celebrations that showcase its vibrant culture and zest for life. The Running of the Bulls in Pamplona, La Tomatina in Buñol, the Holy Week processions in Seville, and the Fallas in Valencia are just a few examples of the exhilarating events that take place throughout the year. These festivities provide an opportunity to witness traditional costumes, music, dance, and the sheer joy of the Spanish people coming together to celebrate.

7. Spanish Architecture:

Spanish architecture is a testament to the country's rich history and artistic achievements. From Roman aqueducts to medieval castles, from Moorish palaces to Gothic cathedrals, and from Renaissance palaces to modernist masterpieces like Antoni Gaudí's Sagrada Familia, Spain offers a diverse range of architectural styles and landmarks. Exploring the architectural wonders of Spain is like embarking on a journey through time and witnessing the evolution of design and construction.

8. Contemporary Spanish Culture:

While Spain's history plays a significant role in its cultural identity, the country is also a vibrant hub of contemporary art, music, and film. Spanish directors like Pedro Almodóvar and Alejandro Amenábar have achieved international acclaim, while Spanish musicians and artists continue to push boundaries and contribute to the global artistic landscape. The contemporary cultural scene in Spain reflects its ongoing evolution and the blending of traditional elements with modern influences.

Exploring Spanish culture and history is a captivating journey through time, encompassing ancient civilizations, architectural marvels, artistic achievements, flavorful cuisine, and exuberant festivals. Spain's cultural heritage is deeply embedded in its people, and their traditions and passions are a testament to the country's rich and diverse tapestry. Whether you're strolling through the streets of Barcelona, savoring tapas in Seville, or immersing yourself in the artistic wonders of Madrid, Spain offers a captivating blend of the old and the new, inviting you to experience its unique culture firsthand.

5

Top Cities and Regions to Visit in Spain

Visiting Spain in 2023 is sure to be an unforgettable experience! With its captivating history, culture, and stunning landscapes, there is no shortage of amazing places to explore. From vibrant cities to quaint towns and picturesque regions, here are some of the top destinations that should be on your itinerary. Get ready to be amazed by all that Spain has to offer!

1. Madrid: The Soul of Spain

As the capital city, Madrid is a must-see destination that displays the country's lively energy and cultural riches. Take in the grandeur of the Royal Palace, wander through the expansive Retiro Park, and visit world-class museums like the Prado Museum and Reina Sofia Museum. Madrid also has a thriving food scene and a lively nightlife, making it an ideal city for both culture buffs and partygoers.

2. Barcelona: The Cosmopolitan Jewel

Barcelona, the capital of Catalonia, is a city overflowing with artistic flair and architectural wonders. Be amazed by the unique designs of Antoni Gaudí, including the iconic Sagrada Familia and Park Güell. Take a leisurely stroll along Las Ramblas, explore the Gothic Quarter, and savor delicious Catalan cuisine. Barcelona's beachfront location adds to its appeal, giving visitors the chance to enjoy both urban and seaside experiences.

3. Seville: Flamenco and Moorish Legacy

Seville, the capital of Andalusia, is a city that radiates charm and passion. Immerse yourself in the rich Andalusian culture by watching a captivating flamenco performance or exploring the vibrant Triana neighborhood. The magnificent Alcázar of Seville, a UNESCO World Heritage site, showcases the city's Moorish influences, while the towering Giralda bell tower offers panoramic views. Don't miss the opportunity to sample traditional tapas and explore the atmospheric streets of the Santa Cruz district.

4. Valencia: A Fusion of Tradition and Modernity

Valencia is a dynamic city that blends history, architecture, and innovation seamlessly. The futuristic City of Arts and Sciences is a must-see, featuring stunning structures such as the Hemisfèric and the Oceanogràfic. Explore the historic center and marvel at the beautiful Valencia Cathedral and the bustling Central Market. Valencia is also renowned for its delicious paella, so be sure to indulge in this iconic Spanish dish during your visit.

5. Granada: The Alhambra and Moorish Splendor

Nestled at the foot of the Sierra Nevada mountains, Granada is a city that takes visitors back in time. The Alhambra, a magnificent Moorish palace complex, is the crown jewel of Granada and a UNESCO World Heritage site. Its intricate architecture and stunning gardens will leave you in awe. Explore the narrow streets of the Albaicín neighborhood, visit the historic Sacromonte district, and experience the vibrant atmosphere of the city's tapas bars.

6. Bilbao: Art, Architecture, and Gastronomy

Bilbao, located in the Basque Country, has undergone a remarkable transformation in recent years. The city's most iconic landmark, the Guggenheim Museum Bilbao, is a masterpiece of modern architecture and home to an impressive collection of contemporary art. Explore the charming Old Town, known as Casco Viejo, and savor the Basque cuisine for which Bilbao is renowned. Don't miss the chance to visit the nearby coastal town of San Sebastian, famous for its beautiful beaches and world-class gastronomy.

7. Malaga and the Costa del Sol: Sun, Sea, and Culture

Malaga, the birthplace of Pablo Picasso, is a city that effortlessly combines sun-drenched beaches with a rich cultural heritage. Visit the Picasso Museum to explore the artist's life and work, and wander through the enchanting streets of the historic center. Malaga's location on the Costa del Sol provides access to stunning coastal landscapes, making it a perfect destination for beach lovers. Nearby, the charming town of Ronda offers breathtaking views from its famous bridge and a glimpse into traditional Andalusian life.

8. The Canary Islands: Tropical Paradise

For those seeking a sun-filled island getaway, the Canary Islands are a dream come true. With their year-round pleasant climate, stunning beaches, and unique landscapes, each island offers its own unique charm. Explore the volcanic landscapes of Lanzarote, hike the rugged trails of Tenerife's Mount Teide, or relax on the golden sands of Gran Canaria. From water sports to nature reserves, the Canary Islands offer a wide range of activities to suit every traveler's preferences.

9. The Balearic Islands: Mediterranean Beauty

The Balearic Islands, including Mallorca, Ibiza, and Menorca, are renowned for their stunning natural beauty and lively party scenes. Mallorca is home to gorgeous beaches, quaint villages, and the bustling city of Palma with its awe-inspiring Gothic cathedral. Ibiza, renowned for its world-class nightlife, also offers tranquil coves and breathtaking sunsets. Menorca, on the other hand, is known for its unspoiled beaches and tranquil landscapes, making it the perfect spot for relaxation and exploration.

Spain is a country that has something for everyone, from art and history to gastronomy and natural beauty. The cities and regions mentioned in this chapter give you a glimpse of the country's amazing offerings. Whether you're exploring the cultural wonders of Madrid and Barcelona, discovering the rich heritage of Andalusia, or soaking up the sun and sea in the Canary Islands or the Balearic Islands, Spain is sure to provide an unforgettable experience in 2023. So, grab your bags, embrace the Spanish spirit, and embark on an unforgettable journey through this magical land.

6

Madrid: The Epitome of Spanish Grandeur and Cultural Magnificence

As the dazzling capital and expansive metropolis of Spain, Madrid rightfully takes its place as the center of the nation's cultural landscape. With its intricate layers of history, vibrant energy, and a timeless charm, Madrid is an irresistible draw for both intrepid travelers and experienced voyagers.

In this chapter, we will embark on a captivating journey through Madrid, uncovering its multifaceted appeal, its many treasures, and the essential information needed for an unforgettable stay in the heart of Spain's shining gem.

1. Historical Overview and Architectural Beauty:

Madrid's history dates back to the ninth century when it was a small Moorish fortress. Over the centuries, it has grown into a major city and the seat of power in Spain during the 16th century. As you explore the city, you will be taken back in time by the many monuments and architectural wonders that are a testament to its rich history.

2. Exploring the Urban Labyrinth:

Let yourself be captivated by the charm of Madrid's urban landscape. Start your journey at the Puerta del Sol, a lively square that is the heart of the city. As you wander through the streets, you will find elegant buildings, inviting cafes, and fashionable boutiques. Don't forget to visit the Plaza Mayor, a grand square that is a great place to relax and enjoy the atmosphere.

3. Museums: Portals to Artistic Transcendence:

Art lovers will be delighted by the many museums in Madrid. The Prado Museum is one of the most famous, with works by Velázquez, Goya, and El Greco. The Reina Sofia Museum is a great place to explore modern and contemporary art, including Picasso's iconic "Guernica". The Thyssen-Bornemisza Museum is also worth a visit, with its impressive collection of art from different eras.

4. Royal Palace and Serene Enclaves:

The Royal Palace is a must-see for anyone visiting Madrid. Its grandeur and opulence will take your breath away. Adjacent to the palace are the Campo del Moro and Sabatini gardens, perfect for a peaceful stroll.

5. Verdant Oasis and Botanical Symphony:

Madrid is full of parks and green spaces that provide a respite from the hustle and bustle of the city. The Buen Retiro Park is a great place to relax, with its gardens, lake, and Crystal Palace. The Casa de Campo is also worth a visit, with its many trails for jogging, cycling, and picnicking.

6. Gastronomic Delights: A Feast for the Senses:

Embark on a gastronomic journey like no other, as Madrid showcases the best of Spanish cuisine. Indulge in the irresistible temptation of tapas, those delicious bite-sized gastronomic creations that will redefine your idea of pleasure. Explore the winding streets in search of traditional taverns and trendy gastrobars, where these culinary masterpieces are crafted with care and presented with love.

Don't miss the chance to savor the iconic Jamón Ibérico, the aromatic chorizo, and the tantalizing patatas bravas. Immerse yourself in a symphony of senses at the bustling Mercado de San Miguel, a vibrant food market that will tantalize you with its array of local specialties and irresistible aromas.

7. Flamenco: The Heartbeat of the Night:

As the sun sets over the city, a nocturnal transformation takes place, bringing Madrid's vibrant nightlife to life. Get ready to be swept away by the captivating allure of flamenco, the transcendent form of traditional Spanish dance.

Venture into the night, where renowned tablaos will enchant you with their unique charms, captivating your senses with every stomp, every strum, and every haunting melody. Afterward, let the city's nocturnal spirit guide you through the intoxicating nightlife districts of Malasaña, Chueca, and La Latina, where an array of bars, clubs, and live music venues will make sure your evenings are filled with memories that will last long after the night has ended.

8. Exquisite Escapes: Day Trips from Madrid:

Madrid's charm is undeniable, but its strategic location also makes it the perfect starting point for captivating day trips to nearby destinations.

7

Barcelona: The Cosmopolitan Gem

Barcelona, the capital of Catalonia in northeastern Spain, is a lively and cosmopolitan city that blends its rich history, stunning architecture, world-class cuisine, and a vibrant arts and cultural scene. It is renowned for its unique Catalan identity, which draws millions of visitors each year who come to explore its captivating attractions and enjoy its lively atmosphere. From the iconic works of Antoni Gaudí to its picturesque neighborhoods and stunning beaches, Barcelona offers a magical experience for travelers looking for a combination of tradition and modernity. In this chapter, we will explore the essence of Barcelona, featuring its must-see attractions, local culture, gastronomy, and useful travel tips for an unforgettable visit to this cosmopolitan gem.

1. A Brief Overview:

Barcelona is a city with a long and fascinating history that dates back over two millennia. It was founded as a Roman colony and grew in importance during the Middle Ages as a prosperous trading city. The Gothic Quarter, with its narrow medieval streets and impressive Gothic architecture, is a reminder of this period. During the late 19th and early 20th centuries, Barcelona experienced a period of economic and cultural flourishing, known as the Catalan Renaixença, which coincided with the Modernisme movement, led by visionary architect Antoni Gaudí.

2. Architectural Wonders:

No trip to Barcelona is complete without exploring its architectural marvels. The most renowned figure in Barcelona's architectural landscape is Antoni Gaudí, whose distinctive style can be seen throughout the city. The crown jewel is the breathtaking Sagrada Família, a magnificent basilica that has been under construction for over a century. Its intricate facades and soaring spires are a testament to Gaudí's genius. Other Gaudí masterpieces include Park Güell, Casa Batlló, and Casa Milà, all of which display his unique blend of nature-inspired elements, vibrant colors, and organic shapes.

3. Exploring the Districts:

Barcelona is a city of diverse neighborhoods, each with its own unique character. The Gothic Quarter, or Barri Gòtic, is a maze of medieval streets that takes visitors back in time. It is home to the Barcelona Cathedral, Plaça Reial, and numerous charming squares and hidden corners. La Rambla, a bustling pedestrian boulevard, is another must-visit area known for its lively atmosphere, street performers, and outdoor cafes.

The modernist district of Eixample is renowned for its wide, grid-like streets and stunning examples of Art Nouveau architecture. Passeig de Gràcia, one of its main avenues, is lined with high-end shops, iconic buildings like Casa Batlló and Casa Milà, and showcases the city's modernist heritage.

For a more bohemian vibe, head to El Raval, a multicultural neighborhood known for its vibrant street art, trendy bars, and alternative cultural spaces. Gràcia, a former independent town absorbed into Barcelona, offers a lively atmosphere with its picturesque squares, local boutiques, and charming cafes.

4. Cultural Offerings:

Barcelona is a city where art and culture thrive. The Picasso Museum houses an extensive collection of the renowned artist's works, providing insight into his early life and artistic development. The National Museum of Catalan Art (MNAC) is another must-visit, showcasing an impressive collection of Catalan art from the Romanesque period to the early 20th century.

Music lovers should not miss the Palau de la Música Catalana, an architectural gem and UNESCO World Heritage site that hosts concerts featuring a wide range of musical genres. The Gran Teatre del Liceu, Barcelona's opera house, offers world-class opera and ballet performances.

5. Culinary Delights:

Barcelona's culinary scene is a paradise for food lovers. From traditional tapas bars to Michelin-starred restaurants, the city offers a myriad of gastronomic delights. Explore the vibrant food markets such as La Boqueria, where you can sample fresh local produce, seafood, and traditional Catalan dishes. Indulge in a traditional paella, fideuà (a Catalan noodle dish), or suquet de peix (a fish stew). Don't forget to try the famous Catalan bread with tomato, known as pa amb tomàquet, and the delightful crema catalana for dessert.

6. Beaches and Outdoor Spaces:

Barcelona's Mediterranean location provides plenty of opportunities to enjoy sun, sand, and sea. The city boasts several beautiful beaches, including Barceloneta, Nova Icaria, and Bogatell, where you can relax, swim, or engage in various water sports. Along the coastline, you'll find an array of beachside restaurants and bars serving delicious seafood and refreshing drinks.

If you prefer green spaces, head to Parc de la Ciutadella, a sprawling park with beautiful gardens, a lake, and the iconic Cascada Monumental. The hill of Montjuïc offers stunning panoramic views of the city, and its attractions include the Montjuïc Castle, the Magic Fountain, and the Olympic Stadium.

7. Festivals and Celebrations:

Barcelona is a city that offers a unique combination of a rich historical background and a modern, cosmopolitan atmosphere. From its awe-inspiring architecture to its vibrant neighborhoods, cultural attractions, and stunning beaches, Barcelona is a destination that has something for everyone. Throughout the year, the city hosts a variety of festivals and celebrations, such as La Mercè, the city's annual festival held in September, featuring street parades, concerts, and fireworks. The Barcelona Grec Festival showcases performing arts, including theater, dance, and music, in various venues across the city during the summer months. Other notable events include Sant Jordi's Day, a celebration of literature and love, and the Festa Major de Gràcia, where the streets come alive with impressive decorations.

No matter what your interests are, Barcelona is sure to captivate you with its charm, cultural diversity, and Mediterranean spirit. Whether you're a history buff, an art enthusiast, a food lover, or simply looking for an unforgettable travel experience, Barcelona is sure to exceed your expectations.

8

Seville: Flamenco and Moorish Heritage

Seville, the capital of Andalusia in southern Spain, is a city that captivates visitors with its lively culture, long history, and remarkable architectural wonders. Flamenco is alive and well here, and the impact of the Moors is still visible in its architecture and customs. In this chapter, we will explore the magical realm of Seville, discovering its flamenco roots and the vestiges of its Moorish past.

Flamenco: The Soul of Seville:

Seville is renowned for its passionate and expressive flamenco performances, which showcase the intense emotions and technical prowess of the dancers, singers, and musicians. To truly experience the soul of the city, attending a flamenco show is a must. The Triana neighborhood, located on the west bank of the Guadalquivir River, is considered the birthplace of flamenco in Seville. Historically, it was a working-class district where the gypsies, who played a significant role in the development of flamenco, resided. Today, Triana is a vibrant neighborhood with many flamenco bars and tablaos (venues hosting flamenco shows) such as Casa Anselma, El Taller Flamenco, and Los Gallos. Besides attending shows, visitors can also explore the Flamenco Museum in Seville, which is dedicated to preserving and promoting the art form. The museum provides valuable insights into the history, styles, and instruments associated with flamenco, allowing visitors to gain a deeper understanding and appreciation for this mesmerizing art.

Moorish Heritage: A Glimpse into the Past:

Seville is a city steeped in history and culture, with a rich Moorish heritage that is evident in its architecture, gardens, and traditions. From the 8th to the 15th centuries, the city was under Moorish rule, leaving an indelible mark on its culture and aesthetics.

The crown jewel of Seville's Moorish heritage is the Alcázar, a stunning palace complex that showcases a blend of Moorish and Christian architectural styles. Its intricate tilework, horseshoe arches, tranquil courtyards, and lush gardens make it a must-see for any traveler. The Patio de las Doncellas (Courtyard of the Maidens) is particularly impressive, adorned with beautiful azulejos (ceramic tiles) and surrounded by elegant arches.

The Giralda Tower is another iconic Moorish landmark in Seville. Originally built as a minaret, it now serves as the bell tower of Seville Cathedral. Ascending the tower offers panoramic views of the city, while its lower levels showcase the architectural elements from the Moorish period.

The neighborhood of Santa Cruz, once the Jewish quarter, also bears remnants of the city's Moorish past. Its narrow, winding streets, whitewashed houses, and charming plazas create a magical ambiance that is reminiscent of the Andalusian Moorish era.

The April Fair (Feria de Abril) is a week-long celebration of flamenco, music, food, and horseback riding that showcases the city's Moorish heritage. The fairgrounds are adorned with brightly colored tents, and locals and visitors alike dress in traditional Andalusian attire, making it a vibrant spectacle.

Seville is a city that offers a captivating journey through time and culture. From the soul-stirring performances of flamenco to the awe-inspiring architecture of the Alcázar and the Giralda Tower, the city immerses visitors in a rich tapestry of art, history, and traditions. Exploring Seville's flamenco and Moorish heritage is a truly transformative experience that should not be missed.

9

Valencia: A Fusion of Tradition and Modernity

Valencia, a charming city situated on the southeastern coast of Spain, is a great combination of old and new. It has a long history, beautiful architecture, a lively culture, and exciting attractions, making it a great destination for travelers of all kinds. Whether you're a history buff, a foodie, an art lover, or just looking for a memorable vacation, Valencia has something for you. In this chapter, we'll take a look at the unique mix of tradition and modernity that makes Valencia so special.

Historical Significance and Architectural Marvels:

Valencia is a city with a rich history that is evident in its impressive architecture. The most iconic landmark is the Valencia Cathedral, also known as the Cathedral of Saint Mary of Valencia. Constructed in the 13th century, the cathedral is a combination of Romanesque, Gothic, and Baroque styles and is a popular pilgrimage site due to its possession of the Holy Grail.

Adjacent to the cathedral is the beautiful Plaza de la Virgen, a square surrounded by historical buildings such as the Basilica of the Virgin and the Generalitat Palace. Exploring the narrow streets of the old town, El Carmen, you will find medieval towers, picturesque squares, and secret spots that tell the story of the city's past.

The City of Arts and Sciences:

Valencia's commitment to modernity is wonderfully demonstrated by the City of Arts and Sciences. This futuristic complex, designed by the renowned architect Santiago Calatrava, is an architectural wonder that displays Valencia's dedication to innovation and modern design. The complex consists of several distinct structures, including the Hemisfèric, an IMAX cinema and planetarium, the Science Museum, the Oceanogràfic, Europe's largest aquarium, and the Palau de les Arts Reina Sofia, an opera house and performing arts center.

The City of Arts and Sciences' avant-garde architecture, with its smooth lines, striking white surfaces, and reflective pools, provides a striking contrast to the city's historic core. Exploring this modern complex is like entering a science fiction movie, giving visitors a glimpse into Valencia's vision for the future.

The Turia Riverbed Park:

Valencia is renowned for its commitment to combining traditional and modern elements, which is exemplified by the remarkable transformation of the Turia Riverbed. In the 1950s, the river was diverted due to a catastrophic flood, leaving behind a dry riverbed. Rather than letting it go to waste, the city chose to convert it into a sprawling park that runs through the center of Valencia.

Today, the Turia Riverbed Park, also known as the Jardines del Turia, is a verdant oasis filled with gardens, playgrounds, sports facilities, and walking and cycling paths. This 9-kilometer-long park provides a tranquil respite from the hustle and bustle of the city, offering locals and visitors alike a place to relax, exercise, and appreciate the outdoors. The park is also home to several noteworthy attractions, such as the iconic City of Arts and Sciences and the picturesque Gulliver Park, where a giant statue of the literary character Gulliver serves as a playground for children.

Gastronomy:

Valencia's culinary culture is a perfect representation of the city's combination of tradition and modernity. The region is renowned for its gastronomic delights, with paella being its most iconic dish. Valencian paella is characterized by its saffron-infused rice, tender meat, and aromatic spices, and is a must-try when visiting the city. You can savor this classic dish in local restaurants or even take a paella cooking class to learn the secrets of its preparation.

Valencia also embraces modern gastronomy trends. The city is home to a vibrant food scene, with a variety of innovative restaurants, trendy cafes, and contemporary tapas bars. You can enjoy creative fusion cuisine that blends traditional flavors with modern techniques, or explore the vibrant Central Market, where you'll find a wide selection of fresh produce, local delicacies, and artisanal products.

Las Fallas Festival:

Valencia's Las Fallas festival is a remarkable event that celebrates the city's passion for both tradition and modernity. Every March, this week-long celebration draws visitors from all over the world. The festival revolves around the construction and burning of intricate sculptures called fallas, which are made of wood, papier-mâché, and other materials. These fallas often satirize current events, celebrities, and political figures, reflecting the Valencians' humorous spirit.

The city is alive with parades, fireworks, music, and traditional costumes during the festival. The streets are filled with the aroma of traditional Spanish food, and the atmosphere is electric. The grand finale of Las Fallas is the "Nit del Foc," or the Night of Fire, when the fallas are set ablaze in a stunning display of light and fire.

Valencia's combination of tradition and modernity creates a captivating atmosphere that attracts travelers from all over the world. Whether you're exploring the city's historical sites, admiring the modern architecture of the City of Arts and Sciences, relaxing in the Turia Riverbed Park, savoring the local cuisine, or experiencing the energy of Las Fallas, Valencia offers an unforgettable travel experience. This city skillfully blends its rich cultural heritage with a progressive outlook, making it a destination that truly has something for everyone.

10

Granada: The Alhambra and Moorish Splendor

Granada, a city located in the Andalusian region of Spain, is renowned for its captivating blend of culture, history, and architectural wonders. One of its most prized attractions is the Alhambra, a UNESCO World Heritage Site and a reminder of the city's Moorish past. Tourists from all over the world flock to the Alhambra to admire its intricate palaces, beautiful gardens, and breathtaking views. In this chapter, we will explore the rich history and captivating charm of Granada, delving into the Alhambra's architectural marvels and its significance in Moorish culture.

1. Historical Significance

To truly appreciate the beauty of the Alhambra, it is important to understand the historical context in which it was built. Granada was once the home of the Nasrid dynasty, the Muslim rulers of the Emirate of Granada. The Alhambra, meaning "the red one" in Arabic, was constructed in the 13th century and served as a fortress, palace, and citadel for the Nasrid kings. It was strategically located on top of the Sabika Hill, offering a breathtaking view of the city and the Sierra Nevada mountains.

2. Architecture of the Alhambra

The Alhambra's architecture is a masterpiece of Islamic art and showcases the exquisite craftsmanship of the Nasrid dynasty. The complex is composed of several palaces, courtyards, and gardens, and it seamlessly blends elements of Islamic, Moorish, and Andalusian design. The intricately carved stucco, geometric patterns, ornate tilework, and delicate arches are a testament to the skill of the artisans who created this luxurious residence. The highlight of the Alhambra is the Nasrid Palaces, including the Mexuar, the Comares Palace, and the Palace of the Lions, each adorned with stunning decorative elements that will leave visitors in awe.

3. The Generalife Gardens: A Relaxing Retreat

Adjacent to the Alhambra, the Generalife Gardens offer a tranquil escape from the grandeur of the palaces. These lush gardens were designed as a place of rest and leisure for the Nasrid rulers. As you wander through the Generalife, you can take in the immaculately groomed lawns, vibrant flowers, and calming fountains. The Patio de la Acequia, with its long pool and rows of cypress trees, is especially captivating. The gardens provide stunning views of the Alhambra and demonstrate the perfect combination of nature and architecture.

4. Cultural Significance

The Alhambra is not only a stunning architectural marvel but also has immense cultural importance. It symbolizes the magnificence of Moorish civilization and serves as a tangible connection to Spain's varied past. The Nasrid dynasty's influence is evident in the intricate details of the palaces and the use of water as a representation of life and purification. The Alhambra's architectural techniques and design elements have also impacted later Spanish and European architecture. The site stands as a reminder of the coexistence and exchange of cultures throughout history.

5. Visiting the Alhambra

A trip to Granada would not be complete without a visit to the Alhambra. This majestic site is renowned for its intricate architecture, stunning gardens, and rich cultural heritage. A visit to the Alhambra offers a unique opportunity to experience the opulence and refinement of the Nasrid dynasty and to immerse oneself in the captivating history of Granada. The Alhambra stands as a testament to the beauty of Islamic art and its enduring influence on architectural traditions.

To make the most of your visit, it is important to plan ahead. Timed entry tickets are required, and it is advisable to book well in advance. Allocating at least half a day to fully experience the Alhambra and its surroundings is recommended. Exploring the various palaces, courtyards, and gardens at a leisurely pace allows for a deeper appreciation of the site's architectural and historical significance. Visiting the Alhambra is an absolute must for any traveler, and it is sure to be an unforgettable experience. The grandeur of the Alhambra and the enchanting allure of its Moorish splendor will leave you in awe.

11

Bilbao: Art, Architecture, and Gastronomy

Nestled in the Basque Country of Northern Spain, Bilbao is a vibrant city that has experienced a remarkable transformation in recent years. Formerly an industrial center, Bilbao has been reborn as a cultural destination, drawing travelers from all over the globe with its unique combination of art, architecture, and gastronomy. In this chapter, we will explore the many captivating aspects of Bilbao that make it a must-see city in Spain.

Artistic Marvels

Bilbao is renowned for its iconic Guggenheim Museum, a stunning architectural feat that has become a symbol of the city's revival. Designed by the renowned architect Frank Gehry and opened in 1997, the Guggenheim Museum Bilbao is a work of art in itself. Its unique titanium-clad curves and modern design stand out against the urban landscape.

Inside, the museum houses an impressive collection of modern and contemporary art. From pieces by renowned artists such as Andy Warhol and Mark Rothko to thought-provoking installations by contemporary artists, the Guggenheim Museum offers a captivating journey through the world of art. The museum's ever-changing exhibitions guarantee that there is always something new and exciting to explore.

In addition to the Guggenheim, Bilbao has a lively art scene. The Fine Arts Museum of Bilbao is another must-see for art lovers. Located in a neoclassical building, the museum displays a vast collection of Spanish and European art, including works by El Greco, Goya, and Van Dyck. The Basque Museum of Contemporary Art (Artium) is also worth a visit, showcasing contemporary Basque art and hosting temporary exhibitions that challenge artistic boundaries.

Architectural Wonders

Bilbao is a city of architectural wonders, with its captivating mix of old and new buildings. The Guggenheim Museum is just one of the many architectural landmarks to explore. The Zubizuri Bridge, also known as the "White Bridge", is a pedestrian bridge designed by Santiago Calatrava that spans the Nervion River and connects the Guggenheim Museum to the old town. Its curved design and white arches make it a popular spot for photographers. The Azkuna Zentroa, formerly known as Alhondiga Bilbao, is a cultural center that was transformed from a wine warehouse into a multi-purpose space by the architect Philippe Starck. It features a glass-bottomed swimming pool and a rooftop terrace, showcasing Bilbao's commitment to innovative architecture. The Euskalduna Palace is another architectural masterpiece, located on the waterfront. It was designed by Federico Soriano and Dolores Palacios and serves as a conference and performing arts center. Its metallic façade and modern design make it a standout structure in the city's skyline. Bilbao is a treasure trove of architectural marvels, and there is much to explore and admire.

Gastronomic Delights

A trip to Bilbao would not be complete without sampling its delicious cuisine. The Basque Country is renowned for its culinary excellence, and Bilbao is no exception. The city has a rich culinary heritage that showcases the region's finest ingredients and traditional cooking techniques.

Bilbao is renowned for its pintxos, the Basque version of tapas. These small, flavorful bites are usually served on skewers or toothpicks and are meant to be enjoyed with a glass of wine or a local Basque cider. The streets of Bilbao are lined with pintxos bars, each offering an array of tasty bite-sized creations. From the classic tortilla de patatas (potato omelet) to the more adventurous combinations of flavors, there is something to please every palate.

For those looking for a more formal dining experience, Bilbao has a plethora of Michelin-starred restaurants. From traditional Basque cuisine to innovative gastronomic creations, these establishments push the boundaries of culinary artistry. Chefs like Eneko Atxa and Martin Berasategui have put Bilbao on the global food map with their creative interpretations of Basque cuisine.

In addition to the traditional pintxos and Michelin-starred restaurants, Bilbao is also home to numerous traditional Basque restaurants known as "sidrerias" and "asadores." These establishments serve up hearty Basque dishes, such as grilled meats and fish, accompanied by locally produced cider or wine. It's a great opportunity to savor the authentic flavors of the region in a cozy and welcoming setting.

Bilbao is a city that combines art, architecture, and gastronomy to create a unique cultural experience. From the awe-inspiring Guggenheim Museum to the architectural wonders that adorn the city's streets, Bilbao offers a feast for the senses. And when it comes to gastronomy, the city's culinary delights are sure to leave a lasting impression. Whether you're an art enthusiast, an architecture aficionado, or a food lover, Bilbao is a destination that will captivate and inspire you in equal measure.

12

Malaga and the Costa del Sol: Sun, Sea, and Culture

Malaga, located on the stunning Costa del Sol in southern Spain, is a destination that perfectly blends sun, sea, and culture. With its glorious Mediterranean climate, beautiful beaches, rich history, and vibrant cultural scene, Malaga offers a unique and unforgettable travel experience. In this chapter, we will delve into the many attractions and activities that make Malaga and the Costa del Sol a must-visit destination in 2023.

1. The City of Malaga:

1.1 Historical Significance:

- Malaga's Phoenician and Roman Origins
   - Moorish Influence and the Alcazaba
   - The Gibralfaro Castle
   - Malaga Cathedral and the Historic Center

1.2 Picasso's Birthplace:

- The Picasso Museum
    - Exploring Picasso's Life and Artistic Legacy
    - Picasso's Birth House and Plaza de la Merced

1.3 Malaga's Modern Transformation:

- The Revitalized Port Area
    - Contemporary Art at the Centre Pompidou Malaga
    - Soho District: Street Art and Urban Culture

2. The Costa del Sol:

2.1 Beaches and Coastal Beauty:

- Marbella's Glittering Coastline
    - Fuengirola and its Family-Friendly Beaches
    - Torremolinos: Vibrant Beach Culture
    - Nerja and the Breathtaking Balcony of Europe

2.2 Outdoor Activities:

- Golfing in Paradise
    - Watersports and Sailing Adventures
    - Hiking in the Natural Parks
    - Cycling Routes along the Coast

3. Gastronomy and Nightlife:

3.1 Traditional Cuisine:

- Malaga's Famous "Espetos de Sardinas" (Grilled Sardines)
    - Tapas and Seafood Delicacies
    - Local Wines and Sweet Malaga Wine

3.2 Dining Experiences:

- Michelin-Starred Restaurants
    - Chiringuitos: Beachside Dining
    - Mercado Central de Atarazanas: Food Market Delights

3.3 Nightlife and Entertainment:

- Beach Clubs and Rooftop Bars
    - Live Music and Flamenco Shows
    - Casino and Nightclubs

4. Day Trips and Excursions:

4.1 Ronda:

- The Spectacular El Tajo Gorge
    - Puente Nuevo: Ronda's Iconic Bridge
    - Ronda's Bullring and Historic Quarter

4.2 Gibraltar:

- The Rock of Gibraltar
    - St. Michael's Cave
    - Apes of Gibraltar

4.3 Mijas Pueblo:

- A Traditional Andalusian Village
    - Donkey-Taxi Rides
    - Panoramic Views of the Coast

5. Events and Festivals:

5.1 Semana Santa (Holy Week):

- Processions and Religious Traditions

5.2 Feria de Malaga:

- A Weeklong Celebration of Music, Dancing, and Flamenco

5.3 Malaga Film Festival:

- A Showcase of Spanish and International Cinema

Malaga and the Costa del Sol provide a captivating mix of sun, sea, and culture. From the historical richness of Malaga's city center to the beautiful beaches and lively nightlife along the coast, this enchanting region has something for everyone. Whether you're keen to discover the artistic legacy of Picasso, savor delicious local cuisine, or just unwind on the sun-kissed beaches, Malaga and the Costa del Sol are sure to make a lasting impression on your 2023 travels.

13

The Canary Islands: An Exquisite Tropical Utopia of Unparalleled Magnificence

Nestled off the mesmerizing northwest coast of Africa, the Canary Islands are a stunning group of sun-drenched volcanic islands, making them one of Spain's most attractive tourist destinations. With a combination of breathtaking landscapes, a temperate climate that offers its blessings all year round, and a variety of ecosystems, the Canary Islands are a tropical paradise, inviting intrepid explorers and those seeking relaxation and natural beauty.

In this article, we will explore the Canary Islands, discovering their unique features, attractions, outdoor activities, and the cultural experiences that await those who visit these heavenly shores. Join us on this extraordinary journey into the captivating world of the Canary Islands!

Geography and Climate:

The Canary Islands, a stunning archipelago, is home to seven main islands, each with its own unique beauty and captivating stories of nature's grandeur and life. These paradisiacal islands, Tenerife, Gran Canaria, Lanzarote, Fuerteventura, La Palma, La Gomera, and El Hierro, are a testament to the incredible power of volcanic activity, with their rugged coastlines and majestic mountains a reminder of the tumultuous eruptions that formed them.

The most impressive of these peaks is Mount Teide, located in Tenerife, which is the highest mountain in all of Spain and has been awarded UNESCO World Heritage status. It is a popular destination for adventurers and nature lovers from all over the world.

The Canary Islands are also known for their wonderful climate, which is mild all year round. Thanks to their ideal location, the winter months are mild and the summer days are balmy, making them a great destination for those seeking the sun's warmth.

The trade winds bring tales of past adventures, providing a gentle respite and filling the air with a sense of peace and enchantment. This creates an ideal atmosphere for outdoor activities and relaxation, making it the perfect place to unwind and rejuvenate.

Natural Wonders:

Embarking on a celestial voyage through the Canary Islands unveils a stunning array of natural wonders, each one captivating and seductive, captivating the senses with their bewildering beauty and extraordinary diversity. From the pristine swathes of sand kissed by the azure embrace of crystalline waters to the verdant havens of lush forests and the awe-inspiring expanse of volcanic formations, the Canary Islands offer a breathtaking spectrum of landscapes, ready to be discovered and treasured.

The Timanfaya National Park, a sanctuary of surreal allure situated in Lanzarote, invites intrepid explorers with its otherworldly tableau. This ethereal landscape was created by the volcanic eruptions that shook the heavens in the 18th century, presenting a barren expanse of solidified lava, replete with dramatic craters and tantalizing geothermal manifestations.

Visitors can take part in guided tours, admiring the sheer majesty of these volcanic wonders, and even witness the raw power of the Earth's molten core at the remarkable "El Diablo" restaurant, where delectable morsels are cooked using the scorching heat emanating from the very bowels of the Earth itself.

For those who love beachfront bliss, the Canary Islands, paragons of coastal enchantment, offer a breathtaking array of ethereal havens, where the golden sands serenade the feet and the crystal-clear waters offer respite from the cares of the world.

Playa de las Canteras, a resplendent shoreline in Gran Canaria, Playa del Duque, an oasis of paradise in Tenerife's captivating allure, and the resplendent Playa de Sotavento, adorning Fuerteventura, are just a few of the countless pristine coastal stretches that beckon and enchant beach lovers from all over the world.

Outdoor Activities:

The Canary Islands are a paradise for the daring explorer, with a variety of landscapes that provide an abundance of exciting outdoor activities. From thrilling adventures to tranquil natural beauty, these islands have something to offer everyone looking to satisfy their craving for adrenaline and serenity.

14

The Balearic Islands: Mediterranean Beauty

The Balearic Islands, situated in the blue waters of the western Mediterranean Sea, are a stunning reminder of the beauty of Spain's coastlines. These four main islands—Majorca, Menorca, Ibiza, and Formentera—offer a variety of landscapes, a deep cultural history, and a lively atmosphere that draws visitors from all over the world. In this chapter, we will explore the captivating charm of the Balearic Islands, discussing their special characteristics, top attractions, and the best ways to appreciate their Mediterranean beauty.

1. Majorca:

The Jewel of the Balearics
- Introduction to Majorca and its geographical features
- Palma de Mallorca: The Capital City
- Serra de Tramuntana: Majestic Mountain Range
- Coastal Gems: Cala d'Or, Alcudia, and Pollensa
- Cultural Heritage: Castles, Cathedrals, and Monasteries
- Beautiful Beaches: Playa de Palma, Cala Mesquida, and Es Trenc
- Outdoor Activities: Hiking, Cycling, and Water Sports

2. Menorca:

A Tranquil Paradise
  - Discovering Menorca's Natural Wonders
  - Mahon: Port City and Cultural Center
  - Ciutadella: Historic Charm and Architecture
  - Pristine Beaches: Cala Galdana, Son Bou, and Macarella
  - Talayotic Sites: Ancient Megalithic Structures
  - Camí de Cavalls: Exploring the Island's Coastal Path
  - Gastronomy: Traditional Menorcan Cuisine

3. Ibiza:

The Party Island and Beyond
  - Introduction to Ibiza's Dual Personality
  - Ibiza Town: Historic Dalt Vila and Modern Entertainment
  - San Antonio: Famous Sunset Strip and Beach Clubs
  - Formentera: A Tranquil Escape
  - Hidden Coves and Turquoise Waters: Cala Salada, Playa d'en Bossa, and Es Vedrà
  - UNESCO World Heritage Sites: Sa Caleta and Dalt Vila
  - Wellness and Spiritual Retreats

4. Formentera:

Paradise on Earth
  - The Serene Island of Formentera
  - Pristine Beaches and Crystal-clear Waters: Ses Illetes, Playa de Migjorn, and Cala Saona
  - Nature Reserves and Marine Life
  - Cycling and Exploring the Island
  - Charming Villages: Sant Francesc Xavier and La Mola
  - Sustainable Tourism Initiatives

5. Sailing and Island Hopping in the Balearics

- Exploring the Archipelago by Boat
    - Itinerary Ideas for Island Hopping
    - Chartering a Yacht or Catamaran
    - Hidden Gems and Remote Anchorages
    - Nautical Activities: Snorkeling, Diving, and Fishing

6. Local Cuisine and Gastronomic Delights

- Balearic Culinary Traditions and Influences
    - Traditional Dishes: Sobrassada, Ensaimada, and Fideuà
    - Seafood and Fresh Mediterranean Flavors
    - Local Wine and Liquors: Hierbas and Palo
    - Farm-to-Table Experiences and Gastronomic Festivals

7. Cultural Festivals and Events

- Celebrating Balearic Traditions and Heritage
    - Sant Joan Festival in Ciutadella, Menorca
    - Sant Sebastià Festival in Palma de Mallorca
    - Ibiza Closing Parties and Music Festivals
    - Formentera's Sant Jaume Festival
    - Traditional Dances, Music, and Fireworks

8. Practical Tips for Travelers

- Best Time to Visit the Balearic Islands
    - Getting to and Around the Islands
    - Accommodation Options: Hotels, Villas, and Agrotourism
    - Language and Communication
    - Health and Safety Considerations
    - Sustainable Tourism Practices
    - Essential Phrases and Cultural Etiquette

The Balearic Islands are a Mediterranean paradise, offering a captivating mix of breathtaking natural beauty, vibrant culture, and exciting entertainment. Whether you're looking for a relaxing beach holiday, a night out on the town, or a chance to explore historical sites, this archipelago has something for everyone. Come and experience the Balearic Islands for yourself and let their Mediterranean charm captivate your senses, leaving you with unforgettable memories of a Spanish island getaway.

15

Northern Spain: Green Landscapes and Coastal Charm

Northern Spain is a region renowned for its stunning natural beauty, verdant landscapes, and captivating coastal allure. With its varied geography, long-standing history, and distinct cultural heritage, this part of Spain provides a magical experience for those looking for a different side of the country. From the craggy mountains of the Picos de Europa to the idyllic beaches of the Cantabrian coast, Northern Spain is a hidden gem just waiting to be discovered.

1. Geography and Climate:

Northern Spain is a region of diverse landscapes, from the Cantabrian Mountains to the fertile valleys and rugged coastline. It is made up of several autonomous communities, including Galicia, Asturias, Cantabria, Basque Country, and parts of Castilla y León and La Rioja. The Atlantic Ocean has a major influence on the climate, making it mild and wet all year round.

2. Green Landscapes:

Northern Spain is known for its lush green scenery, with rolling hills, fertile valleys, and dense forests. The Picos de Europa National Park, located in Asturias, Cantabria, and Castilla y León, is a must-see for nature lovers. This stunning mountain range is renowned for its dramatic peaks, deep valleys, and pristine lakes, making it a paradise for hikers and outdoor enthusiasts.

3. Coastal Beauty:

The region also boasts a stunning coastline along the Bay of Biscay. The Cantabrian coast is dotted with charming fishing villages, picturesque beaches, and rugged cliffs. San Sebastian, located in the Basque Country, is famous for its beautiful sandy beaches, vibrant culinary scene, and elegant promenade. The Playa de la Concha, with its crescent shape and crystal-clear waters, is often regarded as one of the most beautiful urban beaches in the world.

4. Historical and Cultural Heritage:

Northern Spain is steeped in history and culture, with numerous ancient cities and towns preserving their architectural and cultural heritage. Santiago de Compostela, the capital of Galicia, is renowned for its stunning cathedral and is the final destination of the Camino de Santiago pilgrimage route. The old town of Bilbao, in the Basque Country, is home to the iconic Guggenheim Museum, which showcases contemporary art in a striking titanium-clad building.

5. Gastronomy:

Northern Spain is a foodie's dream, with a unique culinary tradition that sets it apart from other parts of the country. The region is renowned for its fresh seafood, including delectable dishes like pulpo a la gallega (Galician-style octopus) and marmitako (Basque tuna stew). Asturias is famous for its hearty cuisine, featuring dishes such as fabada asturiana (bean stew) and cider, which is a traditional drink enjoyed in local cider houses.

6. Festivals and Traditions:

The people of Northern Spain take their festivals and traditions seriously, and visitors have the opportunity to witness and participate in vibrant celebrations. The San Fermín festival in Pamplona, famous for the running of the bulls, attracts people from around the world who come to experience this thrilling event. The Festival of St. James in Santiago de Compostela is another notable celebration, featuring music, dance, and fireworks.

7. Outdoor Activities:

Northern Spain is a great destination for outdoor adventurers. From hiking and mountaineering in the Picos de Europa to surfing on the Atlantic coast, there is something for everyone. The region's rivers and lakes provide opportunities for kayaking, rafting, and fishing, while the mountains offer excellent terrain for rock climbing and paragliding.

8. Wine Regions:

Northern Spain is a paradise for travelers, boasting lush green landscapes, breathtaking coastlines, and a vibrant culture. Whether you're looking for outdoor activities, discovering ancient cities, or simply indulging in the region's gastronomy, Northern Spain offers a unique and unforgettable experience. From the majestic Picos de Europa to the charming coastal towns, this region showcases the diverse beauty that Spain has to offer.

Wine lovers will be delighted to find that Northern Spain is home to several renowned wine regions, where visitors can enjoy wine tastings and vineyard tours. La Rioja, renowned for its red wines, offers stunning vineyard views and charming wineries. The Txakoli wine region in the Basque Country produces crisp and refreshing white wines that pair perfectly with the local cuisine.

16

Southern Spain: Andalusian Delights

Andalusia, located in Southern Spain, is an enchanting place that offers a unique combination of history, culture, and natural beauty. Seville, Granada, and Cordoba are some of the iconic cities in the region, while the Costa del Sol coastline is a great place to soak up the sun. In this chapter, we will discover the many attractions that make Andalusia a must-visit destination in Spain.

1. Exploring Andalusian History and Culture:

Andalusia is a region with a captivating past, shaped by its strategic location and its interactions with different civilizations over the centuries. It was once ruled by the Phoenicians, Romans, Visigoths, and Moors, leaving behind a remarkable cultural legacy. The region is renowned for its Moorish architecture, such as the breathtaking Alhambra in Granada and the Great Mosque of Cordoba. Additionally, Andalusian culture is reflected in its flamenco music and dance, vibrant festivals such as the Feria de Abril in Seville, and traditional culinary delights.

2. Discovering the Soul of Andalusia:

Seville, the capital of Andalusia, is often considered the epitome of Andalusian charm. The city has a vibrant atmosphere with its narrow streets, colorful tiled facades, and lively plazas. The Seville Cathedral, the largest Gothic cathedral in the world, and the Alcázar, a stunning royal palace, are must-see attractions. The iconic Plaza de España and the Triana neighborhood are also worth exploring. Seville's cuisine is a gastronomic delight, with dishes like gazpacho, tapas, and the famous Seville oranges.

3. Uncovering Granada's Moorish Splendor:

Granada, nestled at the foothills of the Sierra Nevada mountains, is a city steeped in Moorish history and enchantment. The Alhambra, a UNESCO World Heritage site, is the crown jewel of Granada. Its intricate Islamic architecture, stunning gardens, and breathtaking views of the city make it an awe-inspiring experience. The historic Albaicín neighborhood, with its narrow streets and Moorish houses, offers a glimpse into Granada's past. The lively atmosphere of the city is complemented by the vibrant tapas culture, where a free tapa is served with every drink.

4. Exploring the Cultural Fusion of Cordoba:

Cordoba, located on the banks of the Guadalquivir River, showcases the cultural fusion of its diverse past. The highlight of the city is the Mezquita-Catedral, a masterpiece of Islamic and Christian architecture. Its mesmerizing forest of columns and red-and-white striped arches leave visitors in awe. Cordoba's Jewish Quarter, with its narrow streets and flower-filled patios, adds to the city's charm. The annual Cordoba Patio Festival, where locals open their patios for public viewing, is a unique cultural experience.

5. Enjoying the Sun, Sea, and More of the Costa del Sol:

The Costa del Sol, stretching along the Mediterranean coast, offers sun-seekers a haven of relaxation. Cities like Marbella, Malaga, and Torremolinos boast beautiful beaches, vibrant beachfront promenades, and a thriving nightlife scene. Marbella's Puerto Banús is a playground for the rich and famous, with luxury yachts, high-end boutiques, and exclusive clubs. Nature lovers can explore the stunning landscapes of the Sierra de las Nieves Natural Park or take a boat trip to the picturesque town of Nerja, famous for its stunning caves.

6. White Villages and Natural Beauty:

Discover the wonders of Andalusia, a region of Southern Spain that is a paradise for travelers. From the vibrant cities of Seville, Granada, and Cordoba to the sun-kissed beaches of Costa del Sol, Andalusia is a place of rich culture and natural beauty. Explore the region's stunning white villages, such as Ronda, Arcos de la Frontera, and Zahara de la Sierra, with their whitewashed houses and narrow streets, and get a glimpse of traditional Andalusian life. Don't miss the Sierra de Grazalema Natural Park and the El Chorro Gorge, where you can take in the breathtaking views of the surrounding landscapes. Whether you are captivated by Moorish architecture, enticed by flamenco rhythms, or seeking relaxation on the coast, Andalusia promises an unforgettable experience. So, don't wait any longer, pack your bags and embark on a journey through this enchanting region of Southern Spain.

17

Basque Country: An Exquisitely Distinct Cultural Odyssey

Nestled between the lush northern reaches of Spain and the picturesque southern expanse of France lies the captivating Basque Country. This region is a tapestry of culture, language, and breathtaking landscapes, making it a truly unique destination for travelers. The Basque Country is a place where the norms of Spain diverge, creating an extraordinary and enthralling realm. Here, one can find a rich history and enchanting traditions that have been passed down through the ages.

The Basque language, Euskara, is one of Europe's oldest tongues and is still spoken today. Our journey through this chapter will explore the very essence of the Basque Country, uncovering its cultural heritage, urban landscapes, tantalizing cuisine, and hidden alcoves full of mystery. Join us as we discover the wonders of this captivating region!

1. Exploring the Secrets of Basque History:

To truly understand the Basque Country, it is essential to delve into its complex historical background. The Basques have left their mark on history, even before the Romans arrived in the Iberian Peninsula. This unique culture is celebrated through the language of Euskara, which is still spoken by its people. To gain a deeper insight into Basque history, one can visit captivating museums, ancient sites with deep-rooted mythology, and vibrant traditional festivals that showcase the strength and resilience of this remarkable region.

2. Bilbao: A City of Art and Innovation:

Bilbao has emerged from its industrial past as a city of art and innovation. It is a place of beauty, with the iconic Guggenheim Museum designed by Frank Gehry standing as a symbol of Bilbao's commitment to art. Inside, visitors can explore a world-class collection of contemporary art, where the tangible and intangible come together. But Bilbao has more to offer than just the Guggenheim. Exploring the winding streets of the Casco Viejo, the city's old town, reveals a glimpse into the past, with traditional pintxos bars, authentic charm, and a vibrant spirit.

3. San Sebastián: A Gastronomic Paradise and Coastal Haven:

San Sebastián is a paradise for foodies, renowned as one of the world's top culinary destinations. Here, visitors can indulge in a variety of pintxos (Basque tapas) and gourmet delicacies in the city's gastronomic sanctuaries. Exploring the Parte Vieja, the city's historic quarter, reveals narrow alleyways full of life. As the day draws to a close, the golden shores of La Concha and Zurriola provide a stunning backdrop for relaxation, surfing, and simply taking in the beauty of the moment.

4. Pamplona: The Magnificence of the San Fermín Festival:

Pamplona, the capital of the Navarre region, is home to the renowned Festival of San Fermín. This week-long celebration in July combines religious devotion with a variety of musical performances. The festival is best known for the Running of the Bulls, a daring pursuit that fills participants with adrenaline. But there is more to the Festival of San Fermín than just the bulls. It is also a chance to experience the culture of Pamplona, with traditional folklore performances and activities that transport visitors back in time.

5. The Basque Coast: Nature's Bountiful Extravaganza:

The Basque Country is a place of enchantment, with its captivating coastal landscapes that stretch out like a celestial vista. Nature's beauty is on full display here, creating a timeless allure that leaves travelers in awe. From the tranquil fishing village of Getaria, whose shores are a sight to behold, to the majestic Flysch cliffs of Zumaia that have stood the test of time, the Basque Coast is a testament to nature's artistry. Coastal towns, with their unique charm, invite explorers to discover their hidden wonders, savor delicious seafood dishes, and take in the breathtaking views of the Bay of Biscay. This rugged paradise is a playground for outdoor enthusiasts, who can explore its trails, ride its waves, and be immersed in the symphony of the elements.

The Basque Country is a place of exploration, with its winding alleys and a wealth of cultural attractions. Bilbao is a hub of artistry and charm, while San Sebastián is a mecca for gastronomy. Pamplona's Festival of San Fermín is a vibrant celebration of culture. Nature's beauty is also on display along the Basque Coast, with its ethereal cliffs, idyllic fishing villages, and pristine beaches. Together, these experiences form a multi-faceted cultural odyssey, inviting curious travelers to explore the Basque Country's enigmatic allure and discover its diverse and captivating landscapes and cultures.

18

Day Trips and Excursions

Exploring the beauty of Spain doesn't just stop at its lively cities and picturesque towns. The country's varied landscapes and rich history provide plenty of chances for thrilling day trips and excursions. If you're a nature lover, a history enthusiast, or just looking for a change of scenery, Spain has a variety of destinations that are perfect for a memorable day trip. In this chapter, we'll look at some of the most fascinating day trips and excursions that will make your Spanish journey in 2023 even more special.

1. Toledo: A Trip to the Past

Just a short drive from Madrid lies the captivating city of Toledo. Known as the "City of Three Cultures," Toledo is a unique blend of Christian, Jewish, and Islamic influences. Its well-preserved medieval architecture and winding streets will take you back in time. Visit the grand Toledo Cathedral, explore the Alcázar fortress, and admire the artworks of El Greco, who found inspiration in this enchanting city.

2. Montserrat: Nature and Faith

Nestled in the mountains, Montserrat is a combination of natural beauty and spiritual significance. Located near Barcelona, this rocky massif is home to the

Montserrat Monastery, a religious site that houses the revered Black Madonna. Take a cable car ride to the monastery, take in the views of the surrounding landscape, and go on scenic hikes to discover hidden chapels and hermitages.

3. Ronda: The Romantic Andalusian Jewel

Perched on a dramatic cliff in Andalusia, Ronda will take your breath away with its views and romantic charm. The iconic Puente Nuevo bridge, spanning a deep gorge, is a sight to behold. Explore the historic bullring, one of the oldest in Spain, and wander through the narrow streets of the Old Town. Don't miss a visit to the Arab Baths and enjoy the beauty of the countryside that surrounds this picturesque town.

4. Costa Brava: Idyllic Beaches and Coastal Splendor

Escape the hustle and bustle of the city and head to the stunning Costa Brava, located along the northeastern coast of Spain. This rugged coastline boasts picturesque fishing villages, secluded coves, and crystal-clear waters. Visit the charming town of Cadaqués, famous for its white-washed houses and its association with Salvador Dalí. Explore the enchanting Cap de Creus Natural Park or relax on the beautiful beaches of Tossa de Mar and Begur.

5. Alhambra and Generalife: Moorish Grandeur

A trip to Spain would not be complete without a visit to the majestic Alhambra and Generalife in Granada. This UNESCO World Heritage site is a masterpiece of Moorish architecture and showcases exquisite palaces, stunning courtyards, and lush gardens. Admire the intricate details of the Nasrid Palaces, wander through the Generalife gardens, and take in the panoramic views of Granada from the Alhambra's fortifications.

6. Caminito del Rey: Thrills and Natural Wonders

For adventure seekers and nature lovers, the Caminito del Rey offers an exhilarating experience. Located in the province of Malaga, this cliffside path winds its way through stunning gorges and offers awe-inspiring views. Originally built for workers of a hydroelectric power plant, it has now become a popular attraction. Put on your hiking shoes, traverse the narrow walkways, and take in the breathtaking beauty of the surrounding landscapes.

7. Santiago de Compostela: The End of the Journey

Santiago de Compostela, located in the region of Galicia, is the final destination of the famous Camino de Santiago pilgrimage route. The city is home to the magnificent Santiago de Compostela Cathedral, where the remains of the apostle Saint James are said to be held. Explore the historic streets, visit the Plaza del Obradoiro, and witness the botafumeiro, a massive incense burner that swings through the cathedral during special ceremonies.

8. Teide National Park: Volcanic Marvels

On the island of Tenerife in the Canary Islands, Teide National Park beckons with its otherworldly landscapes. At its center stands Mount Teide, the highest peak in Spain and a dormant volcano. Take a cable car ride to the summit for panoramic views of the island and its unique rock formations. Explore the park's trails, witness the volcanic activity, and immerse yourself in the surreal beauty of this UNESCO World Heritage site.

9. Córdoba: The Great Mosque-Cathedral

Journey to the city of Córdoba, where the Great Mosque-Cathedral stands as a testament to the city's rich history and cultural fusion. This architectural marvel showcases a blend of Islamic and Christian influences, with its grand mosque transformed into a cathedral. Marvel at the mesmerizing horseshoe arches and explore the picturesque Jewish Quarter, known for its narrow streets and flower-filled patios.

10. Garajonay National Park: A Tropical Forest in the Canary Islands

Explore the lush and ancient laurel forests of Garajonay National Park on the island of La Gomera. This UNESCO World Heritage site is a natural marvel, with its misty forests, vibrant flora, and a captivating atmosphere. Take a hike along the park's trails, listen to the melodies of endemic birds, and immerse yourself in the serenity of this magical place.

If you're looking for a unique experience in Spain, there are plenty of day trips and excursions to choose from. Whether you're interested in history, nature, culture, or simply seeking new adventures, these destinations offer unforgettable memories. Make sure to plan your day trips carefully, consider the distance and transportation options, and make the most of your time to create lasting memories in the beautiful country of Spain.

19

Exploring the Plethora of Outdoor Pursuits in Spain: A Paradise for Adventure Enthusiasts

Spain is a paradise for those who love outdoor activities, with its diverse and abundant landscapes. From majestic mountain ranges to picturesque coastlines, the country offers a playground for those seeking an adrenaline rush and a connection with nature. There is a wide range of captivating experiences to be had in Spain's great outdoors, from invigorating hikes and challenging climbs to exciting water sports and wildlife encounters. Let's take a virtual tour of the amazing outdoor activities that Spain has to offer, highlighting its thrilling adventures and stunning natural beauty.

1. Embarking on Epic Hiking Journeys and Stunning Treks:

Spain is a paradise for hikers, with a vast network of trails that are suitable for all levels of fitness and experience. The Camino de Santiago pilgrimage route is renowned for its spiritual and cultural significance, and it is a popular choice for trekkers who want to experience a combination of natural beauty and historical charm. For those looking for more daring adventures, the Picos de Europa, Sierra Nevada, and Pyrenees Mountains offer stunning views and breathtaking landscapes, making them the perfect backdrop for challenging hikes and unforgettable alpine experiences. The Canary Islands are also a great destination for hikers, with their volcanic terrain and unique flora and fauna.

2. Climbing to New Heights: Conquering Majestic Mountains:

For those who are brave enough to take on the challenge of mountaineering, Spain's majestic mountain ranges are the perfect place to test their endurance and skills. The Pyrenees Mountains, with their awe-inspiring granite peaks, are a popular destination for climbers, who are rewarded with stunning views that will stay with them forever. Closer to Barcelona, the magnificent rock formations of Montserrat are a great spot for traditional and sport climbing, and they provide a great mental and physical challenge.

3. Cycling and Mountain Biking: Unleashing the Pedal Power:

Spain's varied terrain, from coastal plains to soaring mountains, provides plenty of opportunities for cyclists. Those who want to take it easy can explore the sun-kissed Spanish shores, while those looking for an adrenaline rush can go mountain biking in Catalonia, Andalusia, and the Basque Country. The island of Mallorca is a cyclist's paradise, with its well-maintained roads and stunning views, and it has routes for all skill levels.

4. Water Sports: Riding the Waves of Aquatic Excitement:

Spain's extensive coastline, which is bordered by the Atlantic and the Mediterranean, is a great place for water sports. Along the Atlantic coast of northern Spain, surfers flock to the pristine beaches to ride the waves. Tarifa, in the province of Cadiz, is a great spot for windsurfing and kitesurfing, and the Balearic Islands are perfect for sailing, paddleboarding, and diving, with their crystal-clear waters and vibrant marine life.

5. Canyoning and Caving: Unveiling Nature's Hidden Secrets:

Spain's rugged terrain is home to a number of canyons and caves, which are perfect for exploring. Canyoning is a great way to explore majestic gorges, rappel down waterfalls, and take a dip in natural pools. The Sierra de Guara in Aragon and the Sierra de Grazalema in Andalusia are popular destinations for canyoning, and caving enthusiasts can explore the Caves of Drach in Mallorca or the Cave of Altamira in Cantabria, where they can see prehistoric cave paintings.

6. Encounters with Exquisite Wildlife:

Spain is a paradise for outdoor enthusiasts, with its diverse ecosystems and benevolent climate. From conquering soaring peaks to embracing the exhilaration of water sports, Spain offers a realm of infinite adventures. Birdwatching aficionados can marvel at a vibrant avian tapestry in Doñana National Park, while the Sierra de Andújar Natural Park offers a chance to spot the elusive Iberian lynx.

The Strait of Gibraltar, a famed migratory corridor, treats visitors to awe-inspiring avian spectacles and the chance to witness majestic dolphins and whales in their natural habitat. The Pyrenees Mountains harbor a population of brown bears, adding an element of untamed splendor, while the Tablas de Daimiel National Park beckons bird lovers and wetland enthusiasts to marvel at an array of waterfowl and other captivating species.

Come and explore the soul-stirring landscapes, embrace the thrill of adrenaline, and forge unforgettable memories as you partake in the remarkable outdoor activities that grace this enchanting country. Spain is ready to ignite the spirit of adventure within you, and unleash the full breadth of its outdoor splendor.

20

Spanish Cuisine and Gastronomy

The flavors, ingredients, and traditions of Spanish cuisine are renowned around the world. From the lively tapas bars of Barcelona to the classic seafood restaurants of Galicia, Spain offers a unique gastronomic experience. Drawing on its varied regional cultures, historical influences, and abundant natural resources, Spanish cuisine is a celebration of fresh ingredients, simple techniques, and a deep appreciation for food and shared meals. In this chapter, we will explore the exciting world of Spanish cuisine, its iconic dishes, regional specialties, and culinary customs.

A Mosaic of Flavors:

The cuisine of Spain is renowned for its incredible diversity. With 17 autonomous communities and two autonomous cities, each region of the country has its own unique culinary traditions and local delicacies. From the seafood-focused dishes of Galicia to the hearty stews of Castilla y León and the aromatic rice dishes of Valencia, there is something to please every palate.

Tapas: A Spanish Culinary Institution:

No conversation about Spanish cuisine would be complete without mentioning tapas. These small, flavorful plates can range from simple olives and almonds to more elaborate creations like patatas bravas (fried potatoes with spicy tomato sauce) and jamón ibérico (cured ham). Tapas are usually enjoyed with a glass of wine or a cold cerveza (beer) in lively tapas bars, where friends and family come together to share good food and conversation.

Paella: The Pride of Valencia:

Paella is arguably Spain's most famous dish. This saffron-infused rice dish is traditionally cooked in a large, shallow pan and can include a variety of ingredients such as seafood, chicken, rabbit, or vegetables. Paella is a true representation of Spanish cuisine, with its vibrant colors, bold flavors, and emphasis on communal dining. It is often served during festive occasions and gatherings with loved ones.

Seafood Delights:

Given Spain's extensive coastline, it's no surprise that seafood is a prominent part of its cuisine. Coastal regions like Galicia, Andalusia, and Catalonia are renowned for their fresh and flavorful seafood dishes. From Galicia's pulpo a la gallega (Galician-style octopus) to Andalusia's pescaíto frito (fried fish), seafood lovers will be in culinary heaven. Don't forget to try the world-famous Spanish anchovies, prawns, and mussels, which are often served simply with a squeeze of lemon and a drizzle of olive oil.

Traditional Meats and Stews:

Inland regions of Spain also have their own meaty delights. The Castilla y León region is famous for its succulent roast suckling pig (cochinillo) and lamb (cordero), while the Basque Country is renowned for its tender and flavorful beef. Hearty stews like cocido madrileño (Madrid-style chickpea stew) and fabada asturiana (Asturian bean stew) are popular comfort foods, especially during the colder months.

Cheese and Charcuterie:

Spain has a wide variety of delicious cheeses, from the mild and creamy Manchego to the pungent and tangy Cabrales. Cheese lovers will be delighted by the array of options available. Accompanying the cheeses, Spanish charcuterie is a true treat for the taste buds. Jamón ibérico, made from acorn-fed Iberian pigs, is considered a delicacy and is often sliced thinly and served on its own or with crusty bread.

Sweets and Desserts:

No meal in Spain is complete without indulging in some delectable sweets and desserts. From churros con chocolate (fried dough sticks with hot chocolate) to tarta de Santiago (almond cake), Spanish desserts are a delightful combination of flavors and textures. Be sure to try the famous flan, a caramel custard, and the unique turron, a nougat-like sweet typically enjoyed during the Christmas season.

Wine and Spirits:

Exploring the culinary delights of Spain is an exciting experience that offers a diverse range of flavors, colors, and traditions. From the vibrant tapas culture to the paella feasts and regional specialties, there is something for everyone to enjoy. Not to mention the exceptional wines and spirits the country has to offer. Spain is the third-largest wine producer in the world, with a wide selection of varieties, from the full-bodied reds of Rioja to the crisp whites of Rías Baixas.

Sherry, produced in the Andalusian region, is another Spanish specialty. For those who prefer spirits, Spain's national drink, sangria, is a refreshing combination of red wine, fruit, and spirits, while the iconic gin and tonic has gained popularity in recent years. So, why not grab a plate of tapas, raise a glass of Rioja, and savor the extraordinary flavors of Spain? ¡Buen provecho!

21

Festivals and Celebrations in Spain: A Vibrant Tapestry of Culture and Tradition

Every year, millions of people from all over the world come to Spain to experience the vibrant and exuberant festivals and celebrations that take place across the country. From colorful parades and lively music to traditional dances and delicious food, the festivals in Spain offer a unique and unforgettable experience. In this chapter, we will explore some of the most popular festivals and celebrations in Spain, highlighting their significance, customs, and the regions where they take place. Get ready to be amazed by the joyous spirit and infectious energy that pervades the streets during these lively gatherings.

1. La Tomatina

One of the most renowned and unique festivals in Spain is La Tomatina. Taking place on the last Wednesday of August in the town of Buñol, near Valencia, this event involves a massive tomato fight. Thousands of people come together in the streets, armed with tons of ripe tomatoes, ready to engage in a fun and exciting battle, covering the town and its inhabitants in a sea of red pulp. La Tomatina is not only a thrilling experience but also a celebration of joy, freedom, and unity.

2. Feria de Abril

The Feria de Abril, or April Fair, is a vibrant and flamboyant celebration that takes place in Seville, Andalusia. This week-long festival is a showcase of Andalusian culture, filled with music, dance, traditional costumes, and delicious food. The fair begins with an illuminated gateway called the "Portada," and the streets come alive with colorful horse-drawn carriages, known as "casetas," where people gather to dance the Sevillanas, a traditional flamenco dance. The Feria de Abril offers a unique opportunity to experience the charm and passion of Andalusia in all its glory.

3. San Fermín and the Running of the Bulls

One of the most well-known festivals in Spain is the San Fermín festival, held in Pamplona, Navarre. The highlight of this festival is the Running of the Bulls, where daring participants run alongside a herd of bulls through the narrow streets of the city. Although the running itself lasts only a few minutes, the atmosphere leading up to it is electrifying. The festival also includes religious processions, music, dance, and a wide range of cultural activities. San Fermín captures the essence of Spanish courage and excitement, attracting visitors from all over the world.

4. Semana Santa (Holy Week)

Semana Santa, or Holy Week, is a religious festival that takes place in various cities and towns across Spain, with Seville, Malaga, and Valladolid being among the most popular destinations to experience its grandeur. This week-long event commemorates the passion, death, and resurrection of Jesus Christ. Elaborate processions featuring religious statues, ornate floats, and penitents dressed in traditional robes fill the streets, accompanied by haunting music and the aroma of incense. Semana Santa is a deeply emotional and spiritual experience, offering a glimpse into the religious devotion and cultural heritage of Spain.

5. La Fiesta de San Juan

Gatherings and festivities in Spain are an essential part of the nation's culture, giving a special look into its varied customs and history. From the lively disorder of La Tomatina to the solemn parades of Semana Santa, each celebration has its own importance and appeal.

These festivals bring people together, create a feeling of belonging, and let visitors to submerge themselves in the joyous soul of Spain. Whether you like to observe the powerful energy of the Running of the Bulls or the graceful movements of flamenco artists at the Feria de Abril, the festivals in Spain guarantee an extraordinary experience loaded with color, music, and a profound admiration for tradition. So, get your bags ready, join the festivities, and let Spain's lively celebrations captivate you.

On the night of June 23rd, Spaniards celebrate the Fiesta de San Juan, also known as the Midsummer's Eve. This festival marks the start of summer and takes place along the coast, particularly in cities like Barcelona and Valencia. Beach bonfires are lit, and people come together to celebrate with music, dancing, and fireworks. Customs such as jumping over the bonfires or midnight swims in the sea are thought to bring good luck and purify the soul. The Fiesta de San Juan is a lively and enchanting celebration that combines ancient rituals with a festive beach atmosphere.

22

Shopping in Spain: A Multifaceted Retail Extravaganza

When it comes to treating yourself, Spain has an amazing selection of shopping experiences that go beyond just buying things and offer a chance to really immerse yourself in the culture. From the lively streets of Madrid to the chic boulevards of Barcelona, the charming markets of Seville, and the vibrant stores of Valencia, Spain is a paradise for shopaholics. Whether you're looking for designer fashion, unique souvenirs, or traditional crafts, you're sure to have an exciting shopping experience that will delight your senses and give you memories to last a lifetime.

1. Shopping Destinations: Where Dreams Meet Reality

a. Madrid:

As the bustling capital city, Madrid is a paradise for shopaholics looking for the ultimate retail experience. The iconic Gran Vía, with its stunning architecture, is home to a plethora of internationally renowned brands, flagship stores, and upscale boutiques that will satisfy even the most discerning fashionista. For a truly unique experience, explore the enchanting labyrinth of El Rastro, one of Europe's largest open-air flea markets, where you can find antiques, vintage clothing, and exquisite curiosities.

b. Barcelona:

Barcelona is renowned for its avant-garde fashion scene and Passeig de Gràcia is the city's premier shopping street. Here, you can find an eclectic mix of high-end fashion brands, including Chanel, Gucci, and Louis Vuitton. For a more bohemian experience, wander through the narrow streets of the Gothic Quarter, where independent boutiques proudly showcase their unique and artistic creations. And don't forget to visit the vibrant and bustling La Boqueria market, a sensory extravaganza that will tantalize your taste buds with its cornucopia of delectable treats.

c. Seville:

Seville is a city steeped in history and oozing with Andalusian charm. Its picturesque historic center is home to small shops and charming boutiques, where you can find traditional Andalusian crafts, such as exquisite ceramics, delicately crafted fans, and the captivating attire of flamenco. Calle Sierpes and Calle Tetuán are bustling with a lively ambiance and offer a beguiling selection of fashion, jewelry, and unique treasures that tell stories of Seville's storied past.

d. Valencia:

Valencia is a paradise for the epicurean and the discerning shopper alike. The Central Market is a must-visit for food lovers, with its abundant displays of fresh produce, tantalizing delicacies, and aromatic spices. For those with a penchant for luxury, the Colon Market is the place to be, with its curated selection of high-end brands and designer boutiques. And for those looking for unique souvenirs, the Ruzafa neighborhood is the perfect spot, where local artists and artisans display their craft, inviting you to discover one-of-a-kind creations that capture the spirit of Valencia.

2. Traditional Spanish Products: Unveiling the Essence of Spanish Craftsmanship

a. Fashion and Accessories:

Spain has left an indelible mark on the fashion world, with renowned designers such as Balenciaga, Manolo Blahnik, and Amaya Arzuaga. Spanish leather goods, from handbags to shoes, are renowned for their timeless elegance and craftsmanship. Traditional Spanish accessories, such as mantillas and castanets, evoke the flamenco spirit and make for unique and enchanting souvenirs.

b. Ceramics and Pottery:

Spain has a long-standing tradition of ceramics and pottery, which continues to captivate shoppers today. Toledo's Talavera pottery is adorned with intricate designs and vibrant hues, while Seville's Andalusian ceramics reflect the region's vibrant spirit through their kaleidoscope of colors. Valencian ceramics, meanwhile, showcase a delightful fusion of Moorish and Mediterranean influences. These pieces add a touch of artistry to any home and serve as cherished reminders of your Spanish journey.

c. Flamenco Attire:

Experience the passion and allure of flamenco by acquiring traditional flamenco attire. The "trajes de gitana," or flamenco dresses, are characterized by cascading ruffles, vibrant hues, and intricate details, reflecting the intensity and expressiveness of this mesmerizing dance form. Specialized shops in cities like Seville and Madrid offer a captivating selection of flamenco attire, allowing you to take a piece of its fiery spirit home with you.

d. Food and Wine:

Exploring Spain's markets and stores reveals a wealth of delicious treats. Enjoy the robust flavors of high-quality Spanish olive oil, savor the tantalizing aroma of cured meats such as jamón ibérico, and indulge in the nuanced delights of artisanal cheeses. Don't forget to pick up some saffron, the precious spice that adds a touch of Mediterranean magic to any dish, and select a bottle or two of Spanish wine, renowned for its diversity and exceptional quality.

3. Shopping Tips: Navigating the Retail Maze

a. Store Hours:

In Spain, shopping hours usually run from 10:00 a.m. to 8:00 p.m., but it's important to be aware of the siesta tradition, especially in smaller towns and cities. During siesta time, which is usually in the early afternoon, many stores may close temporarily. However, larger shopping centers and department stores usually stay open all day, so shoppers won't be disappointed.

b. VAT Refunds:

Non-EU citizens can get tax refunds on purchases over a certain amount. Look for stores with the "Tax-Free Shopping" logo and get the necessary paperwork to get the refund. Don't forget to keep your receipts and present them at the tax refund counters at the airport before leaving Spain to get your money back.

c. Bargaining:

Bargaining is not common in most stores in Spain, except for flea markets and small independent shops. It's worth asking about discounts or promotions, as you may find some great deals by negotiating.

d. Payment Methods:

Credit and debit cards are accepted in most stores, making shopping easy.

However, it's a good idea to have some cash on hand, especially when visiting small local businesses or markets, where cash may be preferred or even necessary.

e. Duty-Free Shopping:

For those traveling outside the EU, Spain's airports offer duty-free shopping. Take advantage of this chance to find tax-free items, from spirits and perfumes to electronics and designer accessories. Let duty-free shopping add an extra layer of fun and discovery to your trip.

Exploring Spain's shopping scene is an experience like no other. From bustling markets to fashionable streets, you'll be immersed in the country's culture and craftsmanship. Discover unique treasures that will remind you of the beauty and charm of this captivating land. Let the allure of Spain's retail scene bewitch you and make your shopping trip an unforgettable one.

23

Practical Tips for Travelers

Exploring a new country can be an exhilarating and rewarding experience. Spain is a popular destination for tourists from all over the world, with its vibrant culture, rich history, and breathtaking scenery. To make sure your trip is as smooth and enjoyable as possible, it's important to be well-prepared and have some useful advice. In this chapter, we will provide you with a comprehensive guide on practical tips for travelers to Spain.

1. Before You Go:

Before you set off on your journey to Spain, make sure to check the entry requirements for your country. Most visitors from the European Union and Schengen Area don't need a visa to enter Spain, but travelers from other countries may need to get one in advance. Don't forget to make sure your passport is valid for at least six months beyond your intended departure date.

2. When to Visit:

Spain has a diverse climate, so the best time to visit may depend on your preferences and the regions you plan to explore. Generally, the spring (April to June) and autumn (September to November) seasons offer pleasant weather with fewer crowds. If you're looking to enjoy the beach, the summer months (June to August) are ideal, especially in coastal areas. Just keep in mind that certain regions, like Andalusia, can get really hot in the summer.

3. Learn Some Spanish:

Although many Spaniards speak English, it's always helpful to learn a few basic Spanish phrases. Locals will appreciate the effort, and it can make your travel experience even better. Learn simple greetings, thank-you, please, and basic phrases for ordering food and asking for directions. You can also carry a pocket-sized phrasebook or use language learning apps on your smartphone.

4. Money Matters:

The official currency in Spain is the Euro (€). It's a good idea to bring some cash with you, especially for small establishments that may not accept credit cards. ATMs are widely available in cities and towns, so you can withdraw cash in the local currency. Before you go, let your bank and credit card company know about your travel plans to avoid any issues.

5. Safety:

Spain is generally a safe country for travelers, but it's important to take common-sense precautions. Keep an eye on your belongings, especially in crowded tourist areas, and be aware of pickpockets. It's also a good idea to carry a copy of your passport and keep the original document in a safe place. Travel insurance is highly recommended to cover any medical emergencies or unforeseen events during your trip.

6. Healthcare:

Spain has an excellent healthcare system, with both public and private hospitals and clinics. If you're an EU citizen, remember to bring your European

Health Insurance Card (EHIC) to access necessary medical services. Non-EU travelers should make sure they have comprehensive travel insurance that covers medical expenses. It's also a good idea to carry a small first aid kit with essential medications and supplies.

7. Staying Connected:

Staying connected while traveling is essential for navigation, communication, and accessing important information. Consider buying a local SIM card or an international data plan from your service provider to avoid excessive roaming charges. Free Wi-Fi is available in many cafes, restaurants, and hotels, but having a local SIM card ensures constant connectivity.

8. Transportation:

Spain has an extensive transportation network, making it easy to explore different regions. Major cities have well-connected airports, and high-speed trains (AVE) offer efficient travel between cities. For shorter distances, buses are a convenient and cost-effective option. In cities, public transportation systems, such as metros and buses, are reliable and affordable. Consider buying travel cards or passes for unlimited travel within a specific period.

9. Etiquette and Customs:

Spanish culture has its own set of etiquette and customs that are important to be aware of. Spaniards value politeness and respect, so it's important to greet people with a handshake or a kiss on the cheek (depending on the region) and to use "Por favor" (please) and "Gracias" (thank you) frequently. Spaniards also have a more relaxed approach to time, so don't be surprised if things don't run on schedule. Additionally, it's customary to leave a small tip (around 5-10%) at restaurants, cafes, and for taxi drivers.

10. Local Customs and Traditions:

Spain is known for its unique customs and traditions, so it's a good idea to familiarize yourself with them to show respect and fully appreciate the culture. For example, during festivals or religious processions, it's customary to dress modestly and refrain from disruptive behavior. It's also a great opportunity to embrace the local traditions, such as Flamenco dancing, bullfighting, or enjoying siesta (afternoon rest) in some regions.

11. Electrical Considerations:

Spain operates on a 230-volt AC electrical system, and the standard plug type is the European two-pin plug. If your devices use a different plug type or voltage, make sure to bring an adapter or voltage converter to ensure compatibility. Most hotels and accommodations provide universal outlets, but it's still wise to carry a universal adapter for charging your devices on the go.

12. Respect the Environment:

Spain is blessed with natural beauty, so it's important to be responsible and respectful towards the environment. Follow designated hiking trails, avoid littering, and be mindful of water usage. Some protected areas may have specific guidelines, so it's a good idea to familiarize yourself with local regulations and adhere to them.

13. Explore the Local Cuisine:

Spain is renowned for its delicious cuisine, so it's a great opportunity to try local dishes and fully appreciate the culture. Indulge in tapas, paella, churros, and the wide variety of regional specialties. Embrace the Spanish dining culture, which often includes late meals and a leisurely pace. Don't forget to accompany your meals with some excellent Spanish wine or sangria.

14. Cultural Events and Festivals:

Spain is known for its vibrant festivals and cultural events throughout the year. Research and plan your trip around specific festivals or events that interest you. Whether it's the Running of the Bulls in Pamplona, La Tomatina in Buñol, or the Semana Santa (Holy Week) processions, these events offer a unique glimpse into Spanish traditions and can make your trip even more memorable.

15. Pack Accordingly:

Lastly, make sure to pack smartly for your trip to Spain. Check the weather forecast for the regions you'll be visiting and pack appropriate clothing. Comfortable walking shoes are essential, especially for exploring cities with cobblestone streets. Consider bringing a light jacket or sweater, even in summer, as evenings can be cooler. Don't forget essentials like sunscreen, sunglasses, and a reusable water bottle.

24

Language and Communication

Language and communication are of the utmost importance when it comes to travel experiences, especially when exploring the diverse and captivating regions of Spain. Gaining an insight into the language and being able to communicate effectively with the friendly locals can greatly improve your journey and create meaningful connections.

Official Language: Spanish

The official language, which resonates throughout the vast expanses of Spain, is Spanish, and it is often referred to as Castilian Spanish. Spanish, being the primary and predominant medium of communication across the nation, plays an omnipresent and vital role in facilitating seamless and coherent exchanges.

It is crucial to acknowledge that Spanish in Spain exhibits a remarkable degree of variation in terms of pronunciation, vocabulary, and the usage of idiomatic expressions across disparate and diverse regions. For instance, the Spanish spoken in Andalusia may manifest subtle disparities when compared to the linguistic nuances found in Catalonia or the Basque Country.

Regional Languages:

In addition to Spanish, the awe-inspiring tapestry of Spain comprises a plethora of regional languages, each bearing its own distinctive and fascinating history and cultural significance. These regional languages, which hold the esteemed status of being co-official languages in their respective regions, contribute to the rich linguistic and cultural mosaic of Spain. The most prominent and noteworthy regional languages encompass:

1. Catalan:

This captivating and melodious language finds its expression in Catalonia, the Balearic Islands, and Valencia. Catalan, which exhibits elements that resonate with both Spanish and French, has been an integral part of the cultural and linguistic fabric of these areas. Engaging in an earnest and dedicated effort to learn a few rudimentary Catalan phrases can prove to be exceptionally beneficial and endearing when venturing into these regions.

2. Basque:

Embodied by the regions of the Basque Country and certain parts of Navarre, Basque is a language that is as ancient as it is unique. Distinct in its essence and structure, Basque stands apart from any known linguistic relatives. Though acquiring fluency in Basque can prove to be an arduous and formidable task, even demonstrating a modest and genuine attempt to communicate using a few Basque words or phrases can resonate deeply with the local populace and engender a sense of warmth and respect.

3. Galician:

The melodious intonations of Galician grace the scenic and captivating region of Galicia. This enchanting language manifests certain similarities to both Spanish and Portuguese, thereby endowing it with a distinctive and alluring charm. While the majority of Galicians are bilingual in both Spanish and Galician, displaying a genuine interest in their linguistic heritage can serve as a profound gesture of respect and appreciation.

4. Valencian:

Predominantly spoken in the vibrant and diverse Valencian Community, Valencian is closely entwined with the Catalan language. It encompasses its own regional variations and is commonly used alongside Spanish within the region. Familiarizing oneself with a few Valencian phrases can prove to be invaluable when navigating the cultural landscape of this captivating corner of Spain.

Common Phrases:

While it is true that a significant portion of the Spanish populace, particularly those working in the tourism industry, possess a commendable command of the English language or possess a certain level of proficiency, mustering the courage to engage in communication using the native language can go a long way in forging connections and establishing a deeper sense of cultural immersion. Presented below are a selection of indispensable and commonly-used phrases that can serve as a springboard for embarking on a linguistic adventure:

1. Greetings:

- Hola - Greetings and salutations
    - Buenos días - Good morning
    - Buenas tardes - Good afternoon/evening
    - Buenas noches - Good night

2. Polite Expressions:

- Por favor - Kindly or please
    - Gracias - Thank you
    - De nada - You're welcome
    - Perdón/Disculpe - Pardon me or excuse me

3. Basic Questions:

- ¿Dónde está...? - Where is...?
    - ¿Cuánto cuesta? - How much does it cost?
    - ¿Habla inglés? - Do you speak English?
    - ¿Puede ayudarme? - Can you help me?

4. Ordering Food and Drinks:

- Quisiera... - I would like...
    - La cuenta, por favor - The bill, please
    - ¿Tienes algún plato vegetariano? - Do you have any vegetarian dishes?
    - ¿Qué recomiendas? - What do you recommend?

5. Directions:

- ¿Cómo llego a...? - How do I get to...?
    - A la izquierda - To the left
    - A la derecha - To the right
    - Recto - Straight ahead

Tips for Effective Communication:

1. Learn Some Basic Spanish:

Embark on a journey of discovery and mastery by acquainting yourself with common phrases and diligently practicing the rudiments of Spanish before embarking on your trip. This proactive step will not only facilitate seamless and effective communication but will also demonstrate your ardent interest in delving deeper into the cultural tapestry of the region.

2. Use Language Learning Applications:

In this era of technological advancement, a myriad of language learning applications, such as Duolingo, Babbel, or Memrise, are at your disposal. These user-friendly and interactive apps offer meticulously designed lessons and exercises that aim to bolster your linguistic prowess and proficiency in Spanish.

3. Carry a Comprehensive Phrasebook:

Equip yourself with a conveniently-sized and comprehensive phrasebook or download a language translation application that operates offline. This invaluable resource can prove to be particularly advantageous when navigating areas where English speakers are relatively scarce.

4. Embrace the Power of Non-Verbal Communication:

Non-verbal cues, such as gestures, facial expressions, and body language, possess the capacity to significantly augment and amplify your message. However, it is of paramount importance to exercise caution and sensitivity, as certain gestures may bear diverse and contrasting connotations across different cultures. It is imperative to cultivate an attitude of respect and cultural awareness in your non-verbal communication endeavors.

5. Seek Language Assistance:

In instances where language barriers prove to be insurmountable, do not hesitate to seek assistance from those around you. The affable locals, particularly the younger generation, often exhibit eagerness and willingness to lend a helping hand, serving as invaluable interpreters or guides.

6. Engage in Language Exchange Initiatives:

Consider engaging in language exchange programs or forging connections with language partners online. These enriching experiences afford you the opportunity to practice and fine-tune your Spanish language skills with native speakers, thereby providing you with invaluable insights into the local culture and fostering enduring connections.

The realms of language and communication stand as integral and vital components of any travel experience, and this holds particularly true when immersing oneself in the captivating embrace of Spain. While Spanish assumes the mantle of the official language, regional languages resonate with significance and reverence in various corners of the country. By assimilating a repertoire of essential phrases, embracing non-verbal communication, and seeking language assistance when necessary, you can pave the way for seamless and meaningful interactions, thereby imbuing your sojourn in Spain with an indelible and transformative quality.

25

Transportation in Spain

Spain is a vibrant and diverse country with a wealth of cultural heritage, stunning scenery, and bustling cities. It offers a range of transportation options for travelers to explore its wonders. From public transport networks to well-maintained roads and a well-connected rail system, getting around Spain is relatively straightforward. In this article, we will look at the different types of transportation available in Spain, discussing their features, benefits, and things to consider for travelers.

1. Air Travel:

For those looking to travel long distances or visit the stunning Spanish islands, air travel is an excellent option. Spain has a number of international airports, with Madrid-Barajas Adolfo Suárez Airport and Barcelona-El Prat Airport being the busiest. These airports provide connections to destinations all over the world, making them major transportation hubs.

Domestic flights within Spain are also popular, especially for covering large distances quickly. Airlines such as Iberia, Vueling, and Air Europa offer domestic flights, providing convenient connections between major cities and tourist spots. It's important to book in advance to get the best fares.

When flying, travelers should remember to arrive early to complete security procedures. Additionally, it's important to be aware of luggage restrictions and consider the environmental impact of air travel when looking for sustainable transportation alternatives.

2. Trains:

Spain has an extensive and efficient rail network, making train travel a great option for exploring the country. The national rail operator, Renfe, operates high-speed trains known as AVE (Alta Velocidad Española), which connect major cities like Madrid, Barcelona, Seville, Valencia, and Malaga.

AVE trains offer a comfortable and time-efficient way to travel between cities, with speeds reaching up to 300 km/h (186 mph). The trains are modern, equipped with amenities like Wi-Fi, power outlets, and spacious seating. It's advisable to book tickets in advance, especially during peak travel seasons, to secure the desired departure time and avail of discounted fares.

In addition to the AVE network, Renfe operates other types of trains, including regional and suburban trains, which are suitable for shorter distances and connecting smaller towns and villages. These trains offer a more affordable option for travelers on a budget.

3. Buses:

Buses in Spain provide an extensive network, serving both urban and intercity routes. They are an economical mode of transportation and are well-suited for reaching destinations not covered by trains or where train travel may be less frequent or time-consuming.

The bus network in Spain is well-developed, with various operators such as ALSA, Avanza, and Socibus offering comfortable and reliable services. Many buses are equipped with air conditioning, Wi-Fi, and onboard restrooms, ensuring a pleasant travel experience.

It's important to note that journey durations by bus may be longer compared to trains, especially for long-distance travel. However, buses often provide more flexibility in terms of departure times and accessibility to smaller towns and rural areas.

4. Metro and Trams:

Spain's major cities, including Madrid, Barcelona, Valencia, and Bilbao, have efficient metro and tram systems, providing convenient transportation within urban areas. These networks are ideal for exploring city attractions and reaching popular tourist sites.

For example, Madrid operates a comprehensive metro system with several lines covering the city and its outskirts. Barcelona has an extensive metro network as well, complemented by trams that offer a scenic way to travel within the city. Valencia and Bilbao also have efficient tram systems that connect various neighborhoods and tourist spots.

Travelers can purchase tickets for metro and tram journeys from vending machines or ticket offices located at the stations. It's advisable to get a rechargeable travel card if planning to use public transportation frequently, as it offers discounted fares and saves time on purchasing individual tickets.

5. Rental Cars:

Renting a car in Spain provides the freedom to explore remote areas and venture off the beaten path. The country has a well-maintained road network, including modern highways and scenic routes, making it an excellent choice for a road trip.

Rental car agencies can be found at major airports, train stations, and city centers. It's important to have a valid driver's license and be aware of the local driving regulations. In Spain, driving is on the right side of the road, and seat belts are mandatory for all passengers.

When renting a car, it's important to consider the cost implications, including rental fees, fuel, tolls, and parking charges. Parking can be a challenge in city centers, so it's advisable to research parking facilities and consider using public transportation in busy areas.

6. Taxis and Ride-Sharing Services:

Travelling in Spain is easy and convenient, with a range of transportation options available to suit every budget and preference. Taxis are a great choice for shorter distances or when carrying heavy luggage, and can be hailed on the street, found at designated taxi stands, or booked through phone apps. Ride-sharing services such as Uber and Cabify are also available in major cities, offering the convenience of booking rides through smartphone apps and often providing upfront pricing and various vehicle options.

It's important to ensure that the meter is used or agree on a fare before the journey begins, and it's customary to tip the driver around 10% of the fare as a gesture of appreciation. For longer distances, flying between cities or exploring the country by train, bus, or car is a great option. Metro systems are also available in urban areas, making it easy to get around. With so many options available, you can choose the mode of transportation that best suits your needs and make the most of your Spanish adventure in 2023.

26

Exploring the Varied Landscape of Accommodation Options in Enchanting Spain

When planning a trip to the vibrant and diverse country of Spain, one of the most important things to consider is where to stay. This enchanting land is full of culture and stunning scenery, and travelers have a wide range of accommodation options to choose from, depending on their preferences, budget, and travel needs. From luxurious hotels to budget-friendly hostels, from quaint guesthouses to vacation rentals and boutique accommodations, Spain has something for everyone.

1. The World of Hotels: An Unparalleled Haven of Comfort and Convenience

Hotels are a favorite choice for travelers seeking comfort, convenience, and a wide range of amenities. Spain is home to a variety of hotels, from luxurious five-star establishments to more affordable options. Madrid, Barcelona, and Seville are bustling cities with a plethora of hotels to suit different budgets and preferences. Upscale hotels often offer luxurious amenities such as swimming pools, fitness centers, spa facilities, and on-site restaurants. Additionally, most hotels provide essential services such as concierge assistance, round-the-clock room service, and a 24-hour reception.

2. Hostels: A Welcoming Abode for Thrifty Explorers and Social Butterflies

For the budget-conscious traveler and those looking for a friendly atmosphere, hostels are an ideal accommodation option. Spain has a well-developed network of hostels, especially in popular tourist destinations. Hostels are designed to foster a sense of community and offer a variety of lodgings, from shared dormitory-style rooms to private rooms. They also have communal kitchens, laundry facilities, and common areas where people can meet and socialize. Hostels are a great choice for backpackers, solo travelers, and the young at heart.

3. Guesthouses and Bed and Breakfasts: An Intimate Stay in Picturesque Locations

For those seeking a warm and personalized experience, guesthouses and bed and breakfasts (B&Bs) are a great option. These intimate establishments are known for their family-friendly atmosphere and hospitality. Guesthouses and B&Bs can be found in both urban and rural areas. They offer cozy rooms with private en-suites or shared bathrooms, providing a sense of comfort and relaxation. Many of these charming establishments also serve delicious home-cooked breakfasts and provide personalized recommendations and assistance.

4. Vacation Rentals: An Opportunity to Enjoy Homely Comfort and Local Lifestyles

Vacation rentals have revolutionized the travel industry, allowing travelers to stay in fully furnished apartments, villas, and houses. Platforms like Airbnb, HomeAway, and Booking.com offer a wide range of vacation rentals throughout Spain. Renting a vacation home gives travelers the chance to experience the local way of life, enjoy plenty of space and privacy, and take advantage of a fully equipped kitchen and spacious living areas. Vacation rentals are perfect for families, groups of friends, or those looking for a home-away-from-home experience.

5. Paradores: An Unforgettable Stay Steeped in History, Elegance, and Cultural Heritage

Paradores are a uniquely Spanish phenomenon, offering luxurious accommodation in historic buildings such as castles, palaces, monasteries, and convents. These distinctive establishments combine history, culture, and luxury, allowing guests to immerse themselves in the rich heritage of Spain. Each Parador has its own unique character and charm, and a stay in one promises an extraordinary and unforgettable experience, albeit at a premium price.

6. Rural Accommodations: Embracing Tranquility amidst the Idyllic Spanish Landscape

For those seeking to take a break from the hustle and bustle of modern life and immerse themselves in the tranquility of nature, Spain offers a variety of rural accommodations that will captivate the senses. From charming country houses to rustic farm stays and beguiling rural hotels, the country is full of options.

These accommodations are nestled in picturesque locations, offering stunning views of lush landscapes, majestic mountains, and breathtaking stretches of countryside. Not only can you relax and recharge in the embrace of nature, but you can also enjoy a variety of outdoor activities such as invigorating hikes or horseback rides. Plus, many of these abodes offer a delicious selection of traditional regional cuisine, allowing you to sample the gastronomic delights of the region.

7. Boutique Hotels: An Immerse Dive into Distinctive Design and Personalized

Opulence

Exploring Spain requires careful consideration of accommodation options that fit one's budget, preferences, and travel plans. From luxurious to budget-friendly, convivial to extraordinary, Spain offers a variety of options to suit any traveler. Boutique hotels, with their distinctive design, personalized service, and attention to detail, provide a unique and inviting atmosphere.

These intimate havens, often compact in size, offer trendy décor, modern amenities, and bespoke services tailored to meet the needs of their guests. To ensure a successful journey, it is wise to book in advance, especially during peak travel seasons, to guarantee an unforgettable experience in the captivating world of Spanish hospitality.

27

Ensuring Safety and Security: An In-Depth Guide for Travelers Exploring the Vibrant Landscapes of Spain

Before embarking on a journey to the stunning landscapes of Spain, it is important to consider safety and security measures to ensure a worry-free and enjoyable experience. Although Spain is generally considered a safe country, it is still important to take necessary precautions and remain aware of potential risks. In this chapter, we will explore various aspects of safety and security, from personal safety and health to common scams and emergency services.

1. Prioritizing Personal Safety:

- Identifying Safe Neighborhoods and Areas: Delve into an insightful overview of the safest neighborhoods and areas in prominent cities such as Madrid, Barcelona, Seville, and Valencia, ensuring that travelers can navigate their adventures with peace of mind.

- Nurturing Street Smarts: Provide pragmatic advice on cultivating street smarts, including techniques to remain vigilant, avoiding densely crowded locales, and securing personal belongings adeptly.

- Public Transportation Vigilance: Elucidate safety measures for utilizing public transportation systems, encompassing buses, trains, and metro networks, while shining a light on potential risks or scams necessitating awareness.

2. Health and Medical Facilities:

- Essentiality of Travel Insurance: Emphasize the criticality of procuring comprehensive travel insurance that encompasses medical emergencies, repatriation, and contingencies, accompanied by a comprehensive breakdown of selecting an optimal policy.

- Medical Services and Facilities: Pore over the quality of healthcare services in Spain, accessibility to English-speaking medical professionals, and furnish pertinent contact information for emergency medical services.

- Vaccinations and Health Precautions: Foster awareness concerning recommended vaccinations and indispensable health precautions imperative for travelers embarking on their Spanish odyssey.

3. Unveiling Common Scams and Tourist Frauds:

- Thwarting Pickpocketing and Bag Snatching: Unveil the prevalence of pickpocketing incidents in densely populated tourist hubs and empower travelers with astute strategies to stave off theft, thereby safeguarding their personal effects.

- Circumventing Street Vendors and Distractions: Shed light on prevalent scams perpetrated by street vendors, encompassing unwarranted merchandise, distraction tactics, and aggressive sales ploys, encouraging travelers to remain vigilant and alert.

- Mitigating ATM and Credit Card Fraud: Offer invaluable guidance on safeguarding personal information while conducting transactions at ATMs and employing credit cards, underscoring the significance of patronizing secure and reputable locations.

4. Emergency Services and Crucial Contacts:

- Assisting with Police Incidents: Furnish pertinent contact information for the national emergency hotline, local police stations, and elucidate the requisite procedure to report incidents or file police reports.

- Navigating Medical Emergencies: Present an encompassing overview of emergency medical services, helpline numbers, and offer step-by-step guidance on procuring immediate medical assistance.

- Ensuring Consular Support: Enlighten travelers on identifying their country's embassy or consulate in Spain, elucidating the range of services these establishments proffer in the event of exigencies.

5. Natural Disasters and Environmental Concerns:

- Weather Hazards and Mitigation: Delve into weather-related risks across different regions of Spain, expounding upon indispensable advice to remain apprised of weather forecasts and proactively mitigate potential hazards.

- Grappling with Seismic Activity: Spotlight the potentiality of earthquakes, particularly prevalent in specific regions such as the Canary Islands, and extend guidance on preparedness and safety measures.

- Advocating Environmental Consciousness: Foster a sense of environmental responsibility through promotion of sustainable tourism practices, encompassing the respect for natural habitats, water conservation, and waste reduction.

By assimilating an in-depth understanding of safety and security considerations specific to Spain, you fortify your travel experience, minimizing potential risks. Bearing in mind the significance of prudence, you can relish the wealth of cultural, historical, and vibrant tapestries that Spain unfurls. As you embark upon this captivating expedition, rest assured that you have embraced indispensable precautions to ensure an indelible, secure, and memorable journey.

28

Sustainable Travel in Spain

Sustainable travel, also known as ecotourism or responsible travel, is a growing trend worldwide. It emphasizes the conservation of natural resources, the protection of local cultures, and the promotion of economic development in host communities. Spain, with its diverse landscapes, rich cultural heritage, and commitment to environmental conservation, offers abundant opportunities for sustainable travel.

1. Environmental Conservation Efforts:

Spain is renowned for its stunning natural landscapes, from the rugged Pyrenees Mountains in the north to the pristine beaches of the Mediterranean and the volcanic Canary Islands. Recognizing the importance of preserving these ecosystems, various environmental conservation efforts are underway across the country.

a) National Parks and Protected Areas:

Spain boasts a network of 15 national parks and numerous protected areas, such as natural parks and biosphere reserves. These areas safeguard unique habitats and endangered species while offering opportunities for visitors to experience nature responsibly. Examples include Doñana National Park in

Andalusia and Teide National Park in Tenerife.

b) Sustainable Wildlife Tourism:

Wildlife tourism has gained popularity in Spain, particularly for birdwatching. Organizations like SEO/BirdLife promote responsible birdwatching practices and collaborate with local communities to protect bird habitats. The Strait of Gibraltar is a renowned hotspot for migratory birds, attracting nature enthusiasts from around the world.

c) Marine Conservation:

Spain's extensive coastline is home to diverse marine ecosystems. Initiatives like the creation of marine reserves and the promotion of sustainable fishing practices aim to protect marine biodiversity and ensure the long-term health of coastal areas. Cabo de Gata-Níjar Natural Park in Andalusia and the Medes Islands Marine Reserve in Catalonia are notable examples.

2. Cultural Preservation:

Spain's rich cultural heritage is a significant draw for travelers. Sustainable travel in Spain also focuses on preserving and promoting local cultures, traditions, and historical sites.

a) UNESCO World Heritage Sites:

Spain is home to 48 UNESCO World Heritage Sites, including iconic landmarks like the Alhambra in Granada and the Sagrada Familia in Barcelona. Sustainable tourism initiatives at these sites prioritize visitor education, preservation of cultural authenticity, and community engagement.

b) Rural Tourism:

Rural areas offer an opportunity to experience traditional Spanish culture and support local economies. Sustainable initiatives promote responsible rural tourism, including homestays, farm visits, and community-based activities. Villages like Ronda in Andalusia and Cudillero in Asturias exemplify this approach.

c) Gastronomic Tourism:

Spanish cuisine is celebrated worldwide, and sustainable travel in Spain embraces gastronomic tourism that highlights local and organic food production. Farmers' markets, food festivals, and farm-to-table experiences allow travelers to connect with the land, support local producers, and savor authentic flavors.

3. Community Engagement and Social Responsibility:

Sustainable travel in Spain goes beyond environmental and cultural aspects by promoting community engagement and social responsibility.

a) Fair Trade and Crafts:

Many Spanish destinations prioritize fair trade and support local artisans. Visitors can find handicrafts, textiles, and traditional products that directly benefit local communities. Places like Toledo, famous for its traditional sword-making, provide opportunities for travelers to support local artisans and learn about traditional craftsmanship.

b) Volunteering and Conservation Projects:

Numerous volunteer organizations in Spain offer opportunities to participate in conservation and community development projects. These initiatives allow travelers to contribute to local causes, such as reforestation efforts, wildlife conservation, or social development programs.

c) Sustainable Accommodations:

Spain has a range of eco-friendly and sustainable accommodations, including eco-lodges, agrotourism farms, and certified eco-hotels. These establishments prioritize energy efficiency, waste reduction, and the use of renewable resources. Some accommodations even collaborate with local communities to promote sustainable practices and provide employment opportunities.

Sustainable travel in Spain offers a chance to explore the country's natural wonders, delve into its rich cultural heritage, and support local communities. Environmental conservation efforts, cultural preservation initiatives, and community engagement projects are all part of the sustainable travel landscape in Spain.

By choosing responsible tourism practices, travelers can contribute to the preservation of Spain's natural and cultural treasures while creating positive impacts on local economies and communities. So, when planning your trip to Spain, consider sustainable travel options and be a responsible traveler who leaves a positive footprint on the places you visit.

29

Spain for Budget Travelers

Spain is a captivating country known for its vibrant culture, stunning landscapes, and rich history. While it may have a reputation for being a popular tourist destination, it's also possible to explore Spain on a budget. From affordable accommodations to inexpensive dining options and free attractions, this guide will provide you with valuable tips and insights to help you make the most of your budget-friendly journey through Spain.

1. Planning Your Trip on a Budget:

a. Timing your visit:

Consider traveling during the shoulder seasons (spring and fall) when prices for flights and accommodations are generally lower compared to the peak summer season.

b. Research and budgeting:

Create a realistic travel budget by researching the costs of accommodations, transportation, meals, and attractions in the cities or regions you plan to visit. Look for deals and discounts online to save even more.

c. Choosing budget-friendly destinations:

While cities like Barcelona and Madrid are popular, they can also be more expensive. Consider exploring less touristy destinations such as Valencia, Granada, or Seville, which offer a wealth of cultural experiences at a lower cost.

2. Affordable Accommodation Options:

a. Hostels:

Spain has a vast network of budget-friendly hostels that offer comfortable dormitory-style accommodation. They provide an opportunity to meet fellow travelers and often have communal areas and organized activities.

b. Guesthouses and B&Bs:

Opt for smaller guesthouses and bed and breakfasts, particularly in rural areas, as they can offer more affordable rates while providing a unique local experience.

c. Rental apartments:

Consider renting apartments or rooms through platforms like Airbnb or Booking.com, especially if you're traveling in a group or planning an extended stay. This option can be more cost-effective than hotels, and you'll have access to a kitchen for self-catering.

3. Getting Around on a Budget:

a. Public transportation:

Spain has an extensive public transportation system, including buses and trains, which are often more affordable than taxis or rental cars. Research and compare prices to find the most economical options for your itinerary.

b. Discount cards and passes: Look for city-specific discount cards, such as the Barcelona Card or the Madrid Tourist Travel Pass, which offer unlimited public transportation and free or discounted entry to popular attractions.

c. Walking and cycling:

Many Spanish cities have compact city centers that can be easily explored on foot. Renting bicycles is also an inexpensive and eco-friendly way to get around, especially in bike-friendly cities like Seville and Valencia.

4. Budget-Friendly Dining:

a. Tapas and Menu del Día:

Embrace the Spanish culture of tapas, where you can sample small dishes at affordable prices. Look for "Menu del Día" options, which offer a fixed-price menu with several courses, including a drink.

b. Local markets and supermarkets:

Visit local markets like Mercado de San Miguel in Madrid or La Boqueria in Barcelona, where you can find fresh produce, snacks, and affordable meals. Supermarkets are also great for buying picnic supplies or cooking your own meals if you have access to a kitchen.

c. Street food:

Indulge in delicious street food such as churros, bocadillos (sandwiches), or empanadas, which are not only tasty but also budget-friendly.

5. Free and Low-Cost Attractions:

a. Museums and attractions with free admission:

Take advantage of the many museums and attractions in Spain that offer free admission on certain days or during specific hours. For example, the Prado Museum in Madrid offers free entry in the late afternoon.

b. Parks and gardens:

Explore the beautiful parks and gardens that Spain has to offer, including Parque del Retiro in Madrid or Park Güell in Barcelona. These spaces provide a tranquil escape from the bustling cities and are usually free or have a minimal entry fee.

c. Walking tours:

Join free walking tours in major cities like Madrid, Barcelona, and Seville, where local guides offer insights into the city's history and culture. You can contribute with a tip at the end if you wish.

6. Embracing Local Experiences:

a. Festivals and events:

Experience the lively Spanish festivals and events that take place throughout the year, many of which are free to attend. From La Tomatina in Buñol to Semana Santa (Holy Week) processions, these cultural celebrations offer a unique insight into Spanish traditions.

b. Local customs and traditions: Immerse yourself in the local culture by attending flamenco shows, participating in cooking classes, or exploring traditional markets. These experiences are often affordable and provide an authentic taste of Spain.

Traveling to Spain on a budget is an entirely achievable goal with careful planning and a willingness to explore alternative options. By following the tips and suggestions outlined in this guide, you can make your trip to Spain a memorable and affordable experience.

From affordable accommodations and budget-friendly dining to free attractions and unique local experiences, Spain has plenty to offer budget travelers without compromising on the essence of this captivating country. So pack your bags, embrace the adventure, and embark on a budget-friendly journey through the vibrant landscapes and rich cultural heritage of Spain.

30

Unforgettable and Transformative Experiences Await You in Spain

Encompassing a tapestry of history, culture, and breathtaking landscapes, Spain beckons travelers with its myriad of distinctive and awe-inspiring encounters. From immersing oneself in ancient ruins to savoring the epitome of culinary excellence, Spain unravels a plethora of unique experiences, each destined to leave an indelible mark. In this chapter, we invite you to embark on an extraordinary journey as we unveil the hidden gems and unparalleled adventures that await the intrepid traveler in the captivating tapestry of Spain in 2023.

1. Camino de Santiago: A Transcendent Pilgrimage through Time

Prepare to embark on the hallowed path of the Camino de Santiago, an ancient pilgrimage route that has drawn wanderers for centuries. Whether you choose to traverse the well-trodden Camino Francés or explore the lesser-known routes, this spiritual odyssey promises not only to test your physical endurance but also to ignite a soul-stirring transformation. Along the pilgrimage, immerse yourself in bucolic vistas, quaint hamlets steeped in history, and the enduring camaraderie of fellow pilgrims, forging an unforgettable and deeply personal narrative.

2. La Tomatina: Indulge in the Revelry of the World's Most Exuberant Gastronomic Extravaganza

Prepare to be drenched in a riotous symphony of colors and flavors at La Tomatina, an exhilarating festival that has carved its place as the pinnacle of whimsical revelry. Nestled within the charming streets of Buñol, this flamboyant fiesta transcends cultural boundaries as thousands of participants joyously engage in an epic tomato-slinging battle, surrendering to laughter and camaraderie. Unleash your inner child, embrace the pulsating beat of Spain's vivacious spirit, and immerse yourself in this vibrant tapestry of culture and culinary whimsy.

3. Flamenco Immersion in Andalusia: Unleash Your Inner Passion and Surrender to the Rhythms of the Soul

Allow the unadulterated power and emotive force of flamenco to enrapture your senses as you delve deep into the mesmerizing heartland of Andalusia. From the vibrant streets of Seville to the poetic allure of Granada, surrender to the intoxicating pulse of this quintessentially Spanish art form. Enrich your journey by attending captivating live performances, or better yet, participate in intimate flamenco workshops where you will master the intricate footwork and expressiveness, immersing yourself in the very essence of this profound cultural expression.

4. Running with the Bulls: An Adrenaline-Pumping Odyssey Through the Streets of Pamplona

For the daring adventurer yearning to embrace a whirlwind of excitement, the San Fermín festival in Pamplona offers an adrenaline-fueled odyssey like no other. Join the storied tradition of the "Running of the Bulls" as you summon your courage, sprinting through the labyrinthine streets of the city ahead of thundering hooves. This electrifying experience demands agility, audacity, and a zest for life, forging memories that will forever ignite the spark of exhilaration within your soul.

5. Wine Tasting and Epicurean Revelry in La Rioja: A Toast to the Finest Spanish Viticultural Heritage

Venture into the sun-kissed landscapes of La Rioja, an oenophile's paradise where vineyards stretch as far as the eye can behold. Immerse yourself in a sensory symphony as you embark on a captivating wine tour, winding through picturesque landscapes and visiting time-honored wineries, or bodegas. Delve into the secrets

of winemaking, cultivate an appreciation for the delicate nuances of the vine, and indulge in the harmonious marriage of flavors as you savor the resplendent wines that have bestowed global acclaim upon this fertile region.

6. Subaquatic Serenity: Dive into the Enigmatic Realm of the Medes Islands

Embark on an aquatic odyssey of enchantment and discovery as you descend into the azure depths surrounding the Medes Islands. A hidden gem nestled in the embrace of the Mediterranean Sea, these captivating islands offer a gateway to an underwater paradise teeming with vibrant marine life and kaleidoscopic coral formations. Dive beneath the waves, surrender to the embrace of tranquility, and unlock a world of subaquatic wonders that will leave an indelible imprint upon your heart and soul.

Spain, a country brimming with a kaleidoscope of unique experiences, invites you to indulge in unforgettable moments that transcend time and ignite the depths of your spirit.

Whether you choose to embark on a transformative pilgrimage, surrender to the frenzy of a food fight, or immerse yourself in the rich tapestry of Spanish culture, each encounter will weave a tapestry of memories that will forever hold a cherished place in your travel narrative. Set forth on this remarkable

UNFORGETTABLE AND TRANSFORMATIVE EXPERIENCES AWAIT YOU IN...

journey and uncover the treasures that await you in the captivating lands of Spain.

31

Conclusion

As we conclude our exploration of the unique experiences that await you in Spain, it becomes evident that this remarkable country is a treasure trove for adventurous souls seeking unforgettable journeys. From the spiritual awakening of the Camino de Santiago to the exhilarating chaos of La Tomatina, from the passionate embrace of flamenco to the adrenaline-fueled Running of the Bulls, Spain offers a multitude of opportunities to immerse oneself in its rich culture and vibrant traditions.

The landscapes of Spain, from the sun-drenched vineyards of La Rioja to the enchanting depths of the Medes Islands, provide a backdrop for remarkable encounters that engage the senses and leave a lasting impression. Each experience tells a story, connects us to the heritage of this captivating land, and opens a gateway to understanding its people, traditions, and history.

Traveling through Spain in 2023 promises not only exploration and adventure but also moments of self-discovery and personal growth. It is a journey that allows you to step out of your comfort zone, embrace new perspectives, and create cherished memories that will accompany you throughout your life.

Whether you are a pilgrim seeking spiritual enlightenment, a thrill-seeker craving adrenaline-fueled escapades, a culture enthusiast yearning for artistic

CONCLUSION

immersion, or a nature lover seeking solace in breathtaking landscapes, Spain offers a mosaic of unique experiences to satisfy every traveler's desires.

As you plan your trip to Spain and embark on your own adventure, embrace the opportunity to engage with the vibrant culture, indulge in the gastronomic delights, and connect with the warmth and hospitality of the Spanish people. Allow yourself to be captivated by the country's rich history, diverse landscapes, and the unmistakable spirit that pulses through its veins.

In the end, Spain is more than just a destination—it is an invitation to immerse yourself in an extraordinary tapestry of experiences that will leave an indelible mark on your heart and soul. So, pack your bags, open your mind, and let Spain weave its magic as you embark on a journey that promises to be truly unforgettable. ¡Buen viaje! (Bon voyage!)